A NavPress Bible study on the book of

AMOS

A MINISTRY OF THE NAVIGATORS
P.O. Box 6000, Colorado Springs, CO 80934

The Navigators is an international Christian organization. Jesus Christ gave His followers the Great Commission to go and make disciples (Matthew 28:19). The aim of The Navigators is to help fulfill that commission by multiplying laborers for Christ in every nation.

NavPress is the publishing ministry of The Navigators. NavPress publications are tools to help Christians grow. Although publications alone cannot make disciples or change lives, they can help believers learn biblical discipleship, and apply what they learn to their lives and ministries.

ISBN: 0-89109-064-9
10645

Printed in the United States of America

CONTENTS

ACKNOWLEDGMENTS

This LIFECHANGE study has been produced through the coordinated efforts of a team of Navigator Bible study developers and NavPress editorial staff, along with a nationwide network of fieldtesters.

SERIES EDITOR: KAREN HINCKLEY

HOW TO USE THIS STUDY

Objectives

Each guide in the LIFECHANGE series of Bible studies covers one book of the Bible. Although the LIFECHANGE guides vary with the individual books they explore, they share some common goals:

1. To provide you with a firm foundation of understanding and a thirst to return to the book;
2. To teach you by example how to study a book of the Bible without structured guides;
3. To give you all the historical background, word definitions, and explanatory notes you need, so that your only other reference is the Bible;
4. To help you grasp the message of the book as a whole;
5. To teach you how to let God's Word transform you into Christ's image.

Each lesson in this study is designed to take 60 to 90 minutes to complete on your own. The guide is based on the assumption that you are completing one lesson per week, but if time is limited you can do half a lesson per week or whatever amount allows you to be thorough.

Flexibility

LIFECHANGE guides are flexible, allowing you to adjust the quantity and depth of your study to meet your individual needs. The guide offers many optional questions in addition to the regular numbered questions. The optional questions, which appear in the margins of the study pages, include the following:

Optional Application. Nearly all application questions are optional; we hope you will do as many as you can without overcommitting yourself.

For Thought and Discussion. Beginning Bible students should be able to handle these, but even advanced students need to think about them. These questions frequently deal with ethical issues and other biblical principles. They often offer cross-references to spark thought, but the references do not give obvious answers. They are good for group discussions.

For Further Study. These include: a) cross-references that shed light on a topic the book discusses, and b) questions that delve deeper into the passage. You can omit them to shorten a lesson without missing a major point of the passage.

(Note: At the end of lessons two through ten you are given the option of outlining the passage just studied. Although the outline is optional, you will probably find it worthwhile.)

If you are meeting in a group, decide together which optional questions to prepare for each lesson, and how much of the lesson you will cover at the next meeting. Normally, the group leader should make this decision, but you might let each member choose his or her own application questions.

As you grow in your walk with God, you will find the LIFECHANGE guide growing with you—a helpful reference on a topic, a continuing challenge for application, a source of questions for many levels of growth.

Overview and Details

The guide begins with an overview of the book. The key to interpretation is context—what is the whole passage or book *about*?—and the key to context is purpose—what is the author's *aim* for the whole work? In lesson one you will lay the foundation for your study by asking yourself, Why did the author (and God) write the book? What did they want to accomplish? What is the book about?

Then, in lesson two, you will begin analyzing successive passages in detail. Thinking about how a paragraph fits into the overall goal of the book will help you to see its purpose. Its purpose will help you see its meaning. Frequently reviewing a chart or outline of the book will enable you to make these connections.

Finally, in the last lesson, you will review the whole book, returning to the big picture to see whether your view of it has changed after closer study. Review will also strengthen your grasp of major issues and give you an idea of how you have grown from your study.

Kinds of Questions

Bible study on your own—without a structured guide—follows a progression. First you observe: What does the passage *say*? Then you interpret: What does the passage *mean*? Lastly you apply: How does this truth affect my life?

Some of the "how" and "why" questions will take some creative thinking, even prayer, to answer. Some are opinion questions without clearcut right answers; these will lend themselves to discussions and side studies.

Don't let your study become an exercise of knowledge alone. Treat the passage as God's Word, and stay in dialogue with Him as you study. Pray, "Lord, what do you want me to see here?" "Father, why is this true?" "Lord, how does this apply to my life?"

It is important that you write down your answers. The act of writing clarifies your thinking and helps you to remember.

Meditating on verses is an option in several lessons. Its purpose is to let biblical truth sink into your inner convictions so that you will increasingly be able to act on this truth as a natural way of life. You may want to find a quiet place to spend five minutes each day repeating the verse(s) to yourself. Think about what each word, phrase, and sentence means to you. At intervals throughout the rest of the day, remind yourself of the verse(s).

Study Aids

A list of reference materials, including a few notes of explanation to help you make good use of them, begins on page 127. This guide is designed to include enough background to let you interpret with just your Bible and the guide. Still, if you want more information on a subject or want to study a book on your own, try the references listed.

Scripture Versions

Unless otherwise indicated, the Bible quotations in this guide are from the New International Version of the Bible. Other versions cited are the Revised Standard Version (RSV), the New American Standard Bible (NASB), and the King James Version (KJV).

Use any translation you like for study, preferably more than one. A paraphrase such as The Living Bible is not accurate enough for study, but it can be helpful for comparison or devotional reading.

Memorizing and Meditating

A Psalmist wrote, "I have hidden your word in my heart that I might not sin against you" (Psalm 119:11). If you write down a verse or passage that challenges or encourages you, and reflect on it often for a week or more, you will find it beginning to affect your motives and actions. We forget quickly what we read once; we remember what we ponder.

When you find a significant verse or passage, you might copy it onto a card to keep with you. Set aside five minutes during each day just to think about what the passage might mean in your life. Recite it over to yourself, exploring its meaning. Then, return to your passage as often as you can during your day, for a brief review. You will soon find it coming to mind spontaneously.

For Group Study

A group of four to ten people allows the richest discussions, but you can adapt this guide for other sized groups. It will suit a wide range of group types, such as home Bible studies, growth groups, youth groups, and businessmen's studies.

Both new and experienced Bible students, and new and mature Christians, will benefit from the guide. You can omit or leave for later years any questions you find too easy or too hard.

The guide is intended to lead a group through one lesson per week. However, feel free to split lessons if you want to discuss them more thoroughly. Or, omit some questions in a lesson if preparation or discussion time is limited. You can always return to this guide for personal study later. You will be able to discuss only a few questions at length, so choose some for discussion and others for background. Make time at each discussion for members to ask about anything they didn't understand.

Each lesson in the guide ends with a section called *For the Group*. These sections give advice on how to focus a discussion, how you might apply the lesson in your group, how you might shorten a lesson, and so on. The group leader should read each *For the Group* at least a week ahead so that he or she can tell the group how to prepare for the next lesson.

Each member should prepare for a meeting by writing answers for all the background and discussion questions to be covered. If the group decides not to take an hour per week for private preparation, then expect to take at least two meetings per lesson to work through the questions. Application will be very difficult, however, without private thought and prayer.

Two reasons for studying in a group are accountability and support. When each member commits in front of the rest to seek growth in an area of life, you can pray with one another, listen jointly for God's guidance, help one another to resist temptation, assure each other that the other's growth matters to you, use the group to practice spiritual principles, and so on. Pray about one another's commitments and needs at most meetings. Spend the first few minutes of each meeting sharing any results from applications prompted by previous lessons. Then discuss new applications toward the end of the meeting. Follow such sharing with prayer for these and other needs.

If you write down each other's applications and prayer requests, you are more likely to remember to pray for them during the week, ask about them at the next meeting, and notice answered prayers. You might want to get a notebook for prayer requests and discussion notes.

Notes taken during discussion will help you to remember, follow up on ideas, stay on the subject, and clarify a total view of an issue. But don't let note-taking keep you from participating. Some groups choose one member at each meeting to take notes. Then someone copies the notes and distributes them at the next meeting. Rotating these tasks can help include people. Some groups have someone take notes on a large pad of paper or erasable marker board (pre-formed shower wallboard works well), so that everyone can see what has been recorded.

Page 130 lists some good sources of counsel for leading group studies. The *Small Group Letter*, published by NavPress, is unique, offering insights from experienced leaders each month.

BACKGROUND

Amos' World

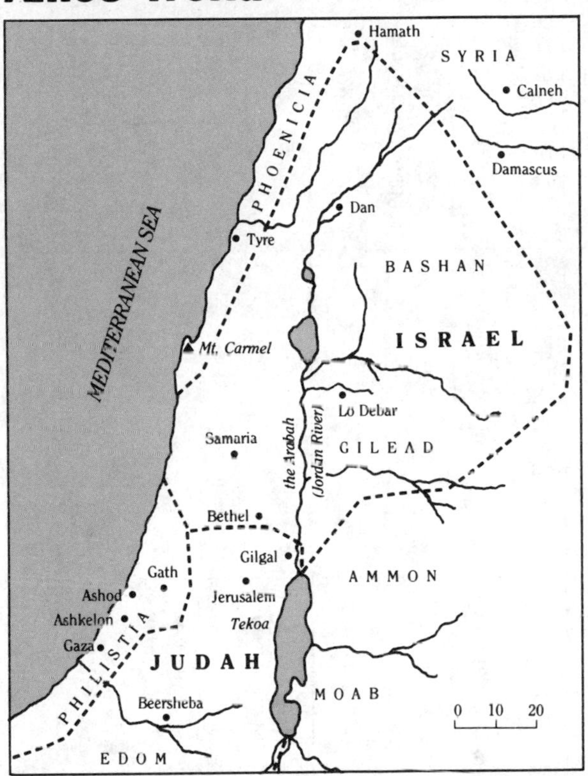

When Amos prophesied warning to Israel, the nation was at the peak of prosperity. Within two decades the nation's strength had crumbled, and within four it was only a memory to those who survived in exile. To his own generation, Amos' words seemed absurd, but the next generation saw too late their tragic accuracy.

Jeroboam I

Israel was a glorious nation under King David and his son King Solomon. But Solomon taxed the nation heavily and instituted forced labor to increase

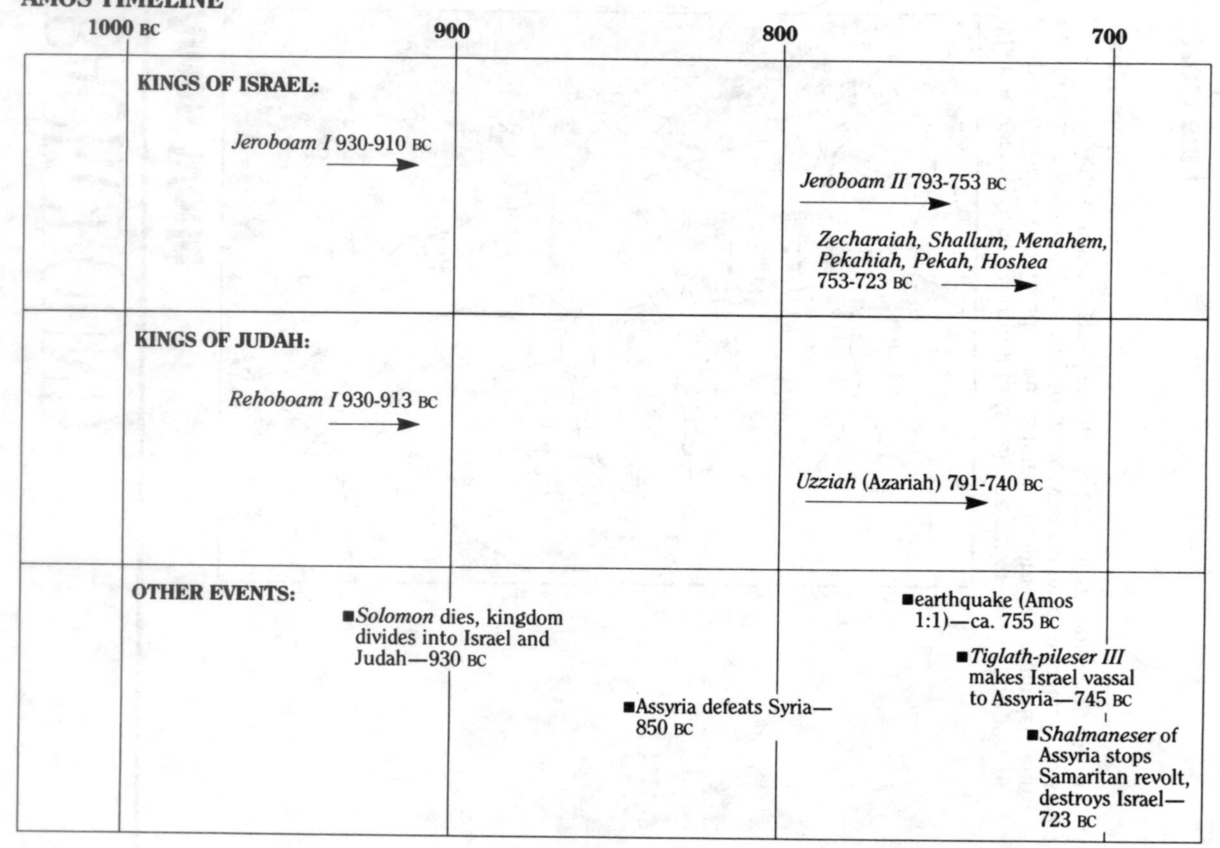
AMOS TIMELINE
1000 BC
900
800
700
KINGS OF ISRAEL:
Jeroboam I 930-910 BC
Jeroboam II 793-753 BC
Zecharaiah, Shallum, Menahem, Pekahiah, Pekah, Hoshea 753-723 BC
KINGS OF JUDAH:
Rehoboam I 930-913 BC
Uzziah (Azariah) 791-740 BC
OTHER EVENTS:
■Solomon dies, kingdom divides into Israel and Judah—930 BC
■Assyria defeats Syria—850 BC
■earthquake (Amos 1:1)—ca. 755 BC
■Tiglath-pileser III makes Israel vassal to Assyria—745 BC
■Shalmaneser of Assyria stops Samaritan revolt, destroys Israel—723 BC

Israel's strength. When Solomon died (about 930 BC), chieftains of the ten northern tribes asked Solomon's appointed heir, his son Rehoboam, to lessen their burden. But Rehoboam refused, for he was inclined to model his kingship on the style of pagan despots rather than on David's style of royal servanthood. Insulted, the northern chieftains chose a northerner named Jeroboam to be Israel's next king. God warned Rehoboam not to lead an army against the rebel north, and in the end Rehoboam was left king of the tribe of Judah, the dispersed tribe of Simeon, part of Benjamin, and some Levites, while Jeroboam ruled the ten[1] northern tribes. Rehoboam's kingdom was thereafter called Judah, while Jeroboam's took the name Israel. The division of the nation was God's punishment on Solomon, for Solomon had contracted dozens of political marriages with pagan princesses, and those wives had led the king to share their pagan practices.

The Lord promised Jeroboam that He would make Jeroboam's dynasty secure if he obeyed the Lord, but Jeroboam did not trust Him. The Law of Moses commanded Israelites to make pilgrimage to the Lord's chosen sanctuary three times a year (Deuteronomy 16:16). Jeroboam feared that if his people continued to make pilgrimage to Jerusalem, they would soon return to Rehoboam. Therefore, Jeroboam set up shrines at Bethel and Dan, declaring that Israel must worship the Lord there. A golden calf stood at each shrine. Pagans commonly mounted their idols on thrones shaped like calves (symbols of power and fertility), and Jeroboam liked the idea of a calf-throne for the invisible Lord. Predictably, the Israelites soon forgot that the calves were thrones and regarded them as idols of the Lord (1 Kings 11:1-12:33).

The religion Jeroboam set up was nationalistic; the king supported his selected priests as the Lord's spokesmen, and the priests supported the king as the Lord's anointed ruler. The religion was also semi-pagan, for the Law of the Lord was increasingly ignored and the people adopted the ideas and practices of their non-Israelite neighbors.

Jeroboam II

The northern nation of Israel was almost constantly at war with one or another of its neighbors for the next 125 years. The nation's productivity was diverted to supporting a large army, and valuable territory was lost to enemies. Then Assyria defeated Aram (Syria) in 805 BC, but so exhausted itself in doing so that neither of those enemies was again a threat to Israel for decades. So when a second King Jeroboam ascended Israel's throne in 793 BC, the time was ripe for Israel to become the dominant nation in the region.

Jeroboam II led his army into the lands Israel had lost since Solomon's time, and eventually took all the conquered area back. Now Israel controlled the major trade routes between Egypt and Assyria, and so the nation began to make money through commerce. However, a powerful few hoarded the profits and even exploited vulnerable fellow Israelites.

Before Jeroboam II, most Israelites had similar standards of living, but now Israel was seeing its first true division of classes. The powerful people began to buy up the land of small farmers, to build large, luxurious homes, and to live like pagan aristocrats. Clever landlords, lawyers, and businessmen used the legal system to wrest property from less powerful and clever people. Vulnerable small farmers became landless hired laborers in semi-poverty. People forgot what God's Law said about a man's personal responsibility for his neighbor. Still, the successful people attributed their wealth to the fact that God had chosen them, and they loved to celebrate the divine favor at their shrines.

Amos

Amos kept sheep in Tekoa (1:1; see the map on page 9), a few miles south of Jerusalem, until the Lord called him to prophesy toward the end of Jeroboam II's reign. Tekoa was a fairly important town in Judah, fortified for defense and in touch with events in the capital, Jerusalem. Amos was no poor hired laborer, but the manager or owner of a small flock. He fed his sheep in part by cutting open and preparing the fruit of the sycamore fig tree (7:14). Thus, Amos was "economically independent"[2] and a respected man in his community, not an outcast engaged in a class struggle against the rich. His book shows that he was well informed about Israel's religious practices, the Law of Moses, historical events in Israel and surrounding nations, and social conditions in Israel. He was not trained as a professional prophet (7:14), but was a devout, informed citizen.

In His mysterious wisdom, the Lord sent a man of Judah, Israel's archrival, to deliver a message from Him to Israel. The message was that Israel was breaking the terms of the agreement (covenant) between the Lord and Israel, and that unless Israel repented, the results of rebellion would catch up with the people.

We may envision Amos as the herald or ambassador of an emperor, sent to a subject nation with a message. The herald travels to the nation's capital, Samaria, to proclaim his message to the nation's leaders (4:1-13, 6:1-14). "Hear ye, hear ye," he says (3:1, 4:1, 5:1). Then he travels to the nation's religious center, Bethel, to speak to the people of all ranks who come there to worship. He gives his message to them, too (7:1-17), and so the whole nation hears it. But the herald is expelled from the nation (7:10). He stays just long enough to see that his duty is discharged, that no one can claim ignorance of the message and lack of fair warning, and he departs. The emperor will invade his rebel land, but the people have been warned.

Amos delivered his message during perhaps just one or two years sometime between 760 and 753 BC. He probably returned to Tekoa to take up his shepherding again and to record his prophecies for future generations.

His mission largely failed, for Israel did not repent. When Jeroboam II died, factions began to tear Israel apart. A strong Assyrian king arose in 745 BC, and Israel soon became a subject of Assyria. More internal strife produced coups and conspiracies, as king after king was assassinated. Finally, an exasperated Assyrian king deported Israel's population to other parts of his empire. The nation Israel ceased to exist (2 Kings 15:8-17:41).[3]

Amos' book

The book of Amos is not one long speech, but a collection of short messages—words from the Lord—delivered on various occasions. These messages, called "oracles" in the Bible (Isaiah 13:1, for instance), are probably not arranged in the order in which Amos spoke them. Rather, Amos has arranged them in a planned order to unfold his message for later generations.

The outline on page 18 divides the book into three sections. Chapters 1-2 pronounce judgment on the nations surrounding Israel and lastly on Israel itself. Chapters 3-6 prove the justice of the Lord's decree about Israel, and offer a last chance to repent. In chapters 7-9, the last chance is past and the Lord declares His standard for judgment; destruction is inevitable, but the Lord gives Amos a glimpse beyond into the restoration of God's people.

A message to us

If the Lord had meant Amos' message only for a nation that would cease to exist in the next generation, He probably would not have had Amos write it down. But the Lord meant it as a message for the Jews who survived Israel's destruction and for Christians in still later centuries. In Amos' prophecy we see important aspects of the changeless character of God, we see God's plan of salvation moving toward its goal, and we see the constant nature of man in need of deliverance from sin. The patience of God, and the awful consequences of rejecting His mercy and patience, are vivid. Even without the book's last four verses, Amos' words leave us seeing ourselves in the people he condemns and praying for Someone to save us from the just consequences of disobedience. But 9:11-15 points toward the gospel—because man has proven unable to abandon sin, God Himself will provide a way for the covenant intimacy between man and God to be restored.

1. The northern tribes are reckoned as ten because Benjamin is counted among them and Ephraim and Manasseh, Joseph's two sons, are each counted as one tribe.
2. Robert Martin-Achard and S. Paul Re'emi, *God's People in Crisis: Amos and Lamentations* (Grand Rapids, Michigan: William B. Eerdmans Publishing Company, 1984), page 4; see also James L. Mays, *Amos* (Philadelphia: Westminster Press, 1969), page 3.
3. For more on this topic, see the box, "Israel after Amos," on pages 88-90.

LESSON ONE

OVERVIEW AND AMOS 1:1-2

The Lord Roars

First impressions

For most of us now, the style of Hebrew prophecy seems foreign and the events that prompted it are unfamiliar. So, the book of Amos can appear to be a string of shouted threats of gloom and doom, and his God utterly unlike the God we know from the New Testament.

But Amos' God is the God of the New Testament, and his message still has much to say to us. In the lessons that follow, you will come to understand the mission of this Old Testament prophet, the times in which he lived, the style with which he spoke and wrote, and the God he served.

For a beginning, read the historical background on pages 9-13, and glance at the timeline on page 10 and the outline on page 18. These will help to orient you to Amos' times and message. Then read through the entire book of Amos in one sitting, to get a general impression of it. Don't worry if many things are hard to understand. Many people find that taking an overview of an unfamiliar book is the most difficult part of studying it, but later they are glad for the foundation. So don't be discouraged; just use as much time and talent as God has provided you.

As you read, you might jot notes for questions 1-4 below.

1. Describe the *mood* (tone of voice, state of mind, feeling) of Amos' words. How does he feel about

For Further Study:
Look for repetition in the following sets of verses: 1:3-2:16.
1:2, 3:8.
3:1, 4:1, 5:1.
3:11, 4:12, 5:16.
5:18, 6:1.
4:6,8,9,10,11.
5:4,14.
2:6-8, 4:1, 5:11-13, 5:24.

God, about his audience, about himself? How does he make you feel his mood? If you think his mood changes anywhere, note where and how it changes.

____

____

____

____

____

____

2. *Repetition* is a clue to the ideas a writer considers most important to his message. What words, phrases, or ideas recur across a section or the whole book?

____

____

____

____

____

____

Study Skill—Style

The style of a piece of writing gives us clues about how to interpret and apply it. We often notice elements of style unconsciously, and we may find it hard to describe a book's style in words. But prophetic books have certain characteristics that make them different from Old Testament history or law. Amos writes differently from the way Paul writes in Romans and the way Jesus speaks in Matthew.

If the idea of style is new to you, consider the following questions:

Does Amos' book seem like a single, unified sermon, or many? Why?

(continued on page 17)

(continued from page 16)

How can you tell that these words were originally spoken aloud?

Does Amos give instructions, reason logically through a topic, appeal to emotions, make predictions, give rebuke, warn, or promise?

How does he use questions, figures of speech, symbolism, and poetry?

Don't worry if you still don't understand what style is. This study guide will point out elements of Amos' style as you go along.

3. What do you notice about the style of Amos' book?

____

____

____

____

____

____

4. What other first impressions of the book do you have?

____

____

____

____

____

Broad outline

Study Skill—Outlining

If your sense of a book is vague after one reading, a broad outline can help to sharpen it. To outline the book of Amos, simply give

(continued on page 18)

(continued from page 17)

titles to each chapter or main section of the book. When you read through, you can probably see where the main breaks in thought are.

Because Amos is an especially difficult book and because you may not be familiar with outlining, the partial outline below is given as an example. You can fill in titles in the blank spaces and expand on the outline as you study each passage in more depth. You might want to leaf through the book now, observing where the outline claims Amos' thought shifts. Since the book has been outlined differently by many different people, you might think about how you would change the sample outline.

- 1:1-2 Introduction
- 1:3-2:16 Eight nations judged
  - 1:3-5 Damascus
  - 1:6-8 Gaza
  - 1:9-10 Tyre
  - 1:11-12 Edom
  - 1:13-15 Ammon
  - 2:1-3 Moab
  - 2:4-5 Judah
  - 2:6-16 Israel
- 3:1-6:14 Four sermons vindicating God's judgment
  - 3:1-15 ______________________________
  - 4:1-13 ______________________________
  - 5:1-27 ______________________________
  - 6:1-14 ______________________________
- 7:1-9:10 Five visions of judgment
  - 7:1-6 Judgment relented
    - 7:1-3 locusts
    - 7:4-6 fire
  - 7:7-9:10 Judgment unrelented
    - 7:7-9 plumb line
    - (7:10-17 challenge from Amaziah rejected)
    - 8:1-14 ripe fruit
    - 9:1-10 at the altar
- 9:11-15 Promise of Israel's restoration

Themes and purposes

Study Skill—Themes and Purposes

It is good in an overview to come to some tentative conclusions about a book's themes and purposes. A *theme* is a main topic that recurs through the book, such as "repentance." A *purpose* is the reason the prophet spoke or wrote, such as "to urge Israel to repent before disaster struck."

Your grasp of Amos' themes and goals may be weak at this point, but you probably have some ideas. Your list of repeated words (question 2) may help you.

5. What are some of the themes and purposes of Amos' prophecy?

The Lord (1:1-2)

6. Amos 1:1 calls the book "the words of Amos," while 1:3,6,9,11,13 reiterates that these are the Lord's words. What do these facts tell you about the nature of prophecy?

For Thought and Discussion: a. What effect does Amos create by repeating the Lord's personal name so often?

b. Why do you think Amos told Israel that the Lord was roaring from *Jerusalem*?

For Further Study: On the lion, see Genesis 49:8-10, Revelation 5:5-6.

The LORD (1:2). The personal name by which God identified Himself to Moses in Exodus 3:14. In Hebrew, which was written without vowels, it is YHWH. It occurs more frequently in Amos' book than almost any other word. It signifies "I AM"—the God who exists in Himself, the God who is actively present. This name—revealed when God saved His people from slavery in Egypt, overthrew His enemies, and made His covenant with Israel—reminded the people of His character as just, mighty, saving, merciful, and faithful to His covenant. (See Exodus 34:6-7; Psalms 103, 111, 146.)

After Amos' day, Jews began to respect God's name as too holy to be pronounced. In speaking and reading Scripture, they substituted a word that means "the Lord." Most English translators render the name "the LORD," while a few guess that it was pronounced "Jehovah" or "Yahweh."[1]

Roars (1:2). To a shepherd like Amos, the most feared creature was the lion, who could attack and devour the flock while the shepherd watched helplessly. The Lord had longed to be Israel's Shepherd, but now He had become Israel's Lion.

7. Amos describes the Lord as a roaring lion in 1:2 and 3:8. What does this image tell you about the Lord?

____

____

____

____

____

Zion (1:2). Jerusalem was built on Mount Zion, and so the two names are used interchangeably in Scripture. To Amos' audience in Israel, Jerusalem was the capital of the arch-enemy, Judah. Israel resented Judah's claim that the Lord authorized sacrifice only at the Temple in Jerusalem. Amos' hearers would have remembered that this man was from near Jerusalem, and they would have chafed at this outsider's criticism.

Pastures . . . Carmel (1:2). The pastures are probably the valleys of Amos' home in Judah. Mount Carmel is the second highest peak in Israel, in the extreme north. So Amos means, "From south to north, from the lowest valley to the highest peak, the Lord's roar blasts like a scorching wind."

For Thought and Discussion: a. Think about the side of the Lord's character portrayed in 1:2. What might lead Him to show this aspect of Himself in our day?

b. How is this aspect of Him consistent with the character He showed in sending Jesus? See, for example, John 2:12-17, Ephesians 2:1-4.

Study Skill—Prophetic Poetry, part one

In ancient times few people could read and books were rare, so most knowledge about religion, law, history, and skills was memorized. Poetry is easier to memorize than prose because it has rhythm, structure, and balance. Therefore, God gave the prophets their sermons in a kind of poetic prose, so that the prophets could remember them and so that the people could not forget them.

Amos 1:2 shows several features of Hebrew poetry. With *synonymous parallelism*, Amos repeats almost the same idea in different words:

> The LORD roars from Zion
> and thunders from Jerusalem. . . .

In *antithetical parallelism*, the second line "contrasts the thought of the first."[2] Hosea 7:14 is an excellent example of this, but Amos 8:8 and 9:3 are somewhat antithetical.

When Amos says,

> the pastures of the shepherds dry up,
> and the top of Carmel withers

he is using a combination of synonymous and contrasting parallelism. His purpose is to intensify the image, to increase the impact by building on the basic idea.

For Thought and Discussion: In what ways is Amos' message applicable to us today? What do we have in common with the people of Israel?

Your response

Study Skill—Application

The last step of Bible study is asking yourself, "What difference should this passage make in my life? How should it make me want to think or act?" Application will require time, thought, prayer, and perhaps even discussion with another person.

At times, you may find it most productive to concentrate on one specific application, giving it careful thought and prayer. At other times you may want to list many implications a passage of Scripture has for your life, and then choose one to concentrate on for prayer and action. Use whatever method helps you to grow more obedient to God's Word.

One question to ask as you try to apply Old Testament Scripture is, "What do I have in common with the original audience of these words?" Even though Christ has died and been resurrected, and even though we have been spiritually reborn, still God's character, His standard of right and wrong, and unredeemed human nature remain the same.

8. a. What is the most important insight you have had from your overview of Amos?

____

____

____

____

b. Is there any way you would like to respond to what you have learned about the Lord? If so, describe what you plan to do.

____

____

____

____

9. If you have any questions about anything in the historical background, this lesson, or the book of Amos, write them down. You could share them with your study group, pursue answers in one of the sources on pages 127-131, ask someone knowledgeable, or wait to see if you can answer them after further study.

____

____

____

____

____

____

Optional Application: Choose something from your first reading of Amos to meditate on for the next week, something that especially strikes you. For example, you could meditate on the Lord as a Lion roaring at His people (1:2). What implications does this side of Him have for your life? How does His character motivate you to treat Him and other people?

Look at page 7 for some suggestions about meditating. Some other verses to consider are 5:14-15, 5:24, and 6:1.

For the group

This "For the group" section and the ones in later lessons are intended to suggest ways of structuring your discussions. Feel free to select what suits your group. The main goals of this lesson are to get to know the book of Amos in general and to get to know the people with whom you are going to study the book.

Worship. Some groups like to begin with prayer and/or singing. Some share requests for prayer at the beginning but leave the actual prayer until after the study. Others prefer just to chat and have refreshments for a while and then move to the study, leaving worship until the end.

Warm-up. The beginning of a new study is a good time to lay a foundation for honest sharing of ideas, to get comfortable with each other, and to encourage a sense of common purpose. One way to establish common ground is to talk about what each group member hopes to get out of your group—out of your study of Amos, and out of any prayer, singing, sharing, outreach, or anything else you might do together. If you have someone write down each member's hopes and expectations, then you can look back at these goals later to see if they are being met.

You may decide to take fifteen minutes or so at the beginning of your discussion of lesson one for this topic. Or, you may decide to take a whole meeting just to introduce the study, to hand out books, and to discuss your expectations.

Reading. It is usually helpful to read the passage you are going to discuss aloud before you talk about it. However, you probably won't want to read all of Amos aloud. You could refresh everyone's memory by taking turns reading brief portions, such as 1:1-2, 1:3, 2:6-8, 3:1-2, 3:8, 4:1-3, 4:11, 4:12-13, 5:1-2, 5:18, 6:1, 7:7-8, 8:1-2, and 9:11-15.

First impressions. Give everyone a chance to voice his or her first impressions of Amos' mood, style, etc. (questions 1-4). Make a list of repeated words and ideas (question 2), and then discuss the book's themes and purposes (question 5). You may need to discuss what *mood* and *style* are briefly, or you may find it most effective to point out places where Amos shows some part of his style or the Lord's mood. For instance, in 1:2 and 2:6-16 the Lord sounds angry, and in 5:1-3 He grieves. In 1:2 Amos uses parallelism and metaphors (figures of speech), and in 3:3-6 he uses questions. In 4:4, 6:2, and 7:16 he quotes his audience. Don't belabor this issue of style, just plant the idea in everyone's mind. Style and mood are clues to how Amos' message is like and unlike Isaiah's or Jeremiah's.

Since Amos is a difficult book, urge the group to ask questions about anything in the study guide or the book itself. Instead of answering every question right away, you may decide to write them down. The group may be able to answer questions later after studying in more detail.

You might leaf through the book together, comparing it to the outline on page 18. Do you see the various parts of the book?

The Lord. The Lord presents a fierce side of His character in Amos' prophecy. Summarize how He appears in your first reading, especially in 1:2. To some people He seems very different from the God of the New Testament, but how does this side of Him show why Jesus' death was necessary? As you study Amos, it will be important to keep connecting this book with the New Testament, so that Christians can see how God's character and plan are consistent.

Your response. You may find it difficult to come up with specific applications after an overview of Amos, especially if you are not used to making specific applications after studying a passage. If the idea is new to some members of the group, you might try thinking of some examples together. First name some general ways in which Amos is applicable today, and then move to some specific ways you might act, think, or pray in response. Try some of the optional questions to stimulate thought.

Wrap up. The group leader should have read through lesson two and its "For the group" section. At this point, he or she might give a short summary of what members can expect in that lesson and in the coming meeting. This is a chance to whet everyone's appetite, assign any optional questions, omit any numbered questions, or forewarn members of possible difficulties.

You might also encourage any members who found the overview especially hard. Some people are better at seeing the big picture or the whole of a book than others. Some are best at analyzing a particular verse or paragraph, while others are strongest at seeing how a passage applies to our lives. Urge members to give thanks for their own and others' strengths, and to give and request help when needed. The group is a place to learn from each other. Later lessons will draw on the gifts of close analyzers as well as overviewers and appliers, practical as well as theoretical thinkers.

Worship. You might spend some time at the end of your meeting praising the Lord for who He is—the LORD, the I AM, the Lion.

Old Testament Prophets, part one

The Hebrew word, "prophet" (*nabi*) comes from the verb "to call" (*nabu*). It indicates that the prophet was uniquely called to be intimate with the Lord and to speak for Him. A related word is "seer," one who "sees" the plans and judgments of the Lord.

There had been prophets in Israel ever since the Lord gave Moses the Law on Mount Sinai.

(continued on page 26)

(continued from page 25)

Moses was the first prophet, and just before his death he promised that Israel would have a series of prophets after him (Deuteronomy 18:14-22).[3] The prophets' main job "was to *speak* for God to their own contemporaries."[4]

Thus, prediction of events in the far future was often not a prophet's task. More often, he told forth the Lord's assessment of the current situation in Israel or Judah, and foretold how the Lord planned to respond.

The prophets were not radical social and religious thinkers transforming Israel's faith. Rather, the covenant agreement was the standard for justice and religion from Moses through Malachi.

(continued on page 46)

1. J. A. Motyer, "The Names of God," *Eerdman's Handbook to the Bible*, edited by David Alexander and Pat Alexander (Grand Rapids, Michigan: William B. Eerdmans Publishing Company, 1973), pages 157-158. (This work is not cited again.)
2. Gordon Fee and Douglas Stuart, *How to Read the Bible for All Its Worth* (Grand Rapids, Michigan: Zondervan Corporation, 1984), page 162.
3. *The NIV Study Bible*, edited by Kenneth Barker (Grand Rapids, Michigan: Zondervan Corporation, 1985), page 267.
4. Fee and Stuart, page 150.

LESSON TWO

AMOS 1:3-2:3

The Nations Judged

In 1:3-2:16, Amos condemns each of the nations surrounding Israel, beginning with the pagan nations, turning then to Judah, and finally coming home to Israel itself.

Read through 1:3-2:3 at least once before beginning the questions. As you read, think about why Amos began his indictment of Israel with judgments upon the pagans, who had never received the Lord's covenant.

For three sins, . . . even for four (1:3,6,9,11,13; 2:1,4,6). This Hebrew idiom means that a careful count (in this case, a count of a nation's sins) has been taken, and the result is reliable. Up through the "third sin" the Lord has been patient, but the "fourth sin" is what we would call the last straw.[1]

Damascus (1:3). The capital of Aram (Syria). ***Hazael*** became king of Aram in 842 by murdering King Ben-Hadad I. He conquered and brutally abused Israel's territory east of the Jordan River, including ***Gilead***. On how he "threshed" Gilead, see 2 Kings 8:7-15; 10:32-33; 13:3,7,22-25.

Hazael's son, ***Ben-Hadad II***, succeeded him in 796 or 806 BC.[2] Israel was able to reconquer some of its lost territory from Ben-Hadad, but Gilead remained under the Aramean yoke for several more decades.

For Thought and Discussion: Amos predicts the same consequence for each nation's sin (1:4,7,10,12,14; 2:2,5). What is that consequence, and why is it appropriate?

Threshed (1:3). When barley was harvested, the cut stalks had to be threshed to separate the grain from the straw. This was often done by driving a wooden sledge with sharp teeth over the cut stalks. Amos may have been using a metaphor—a figure of speech—to depict Hazael's brutal methods of conquest (see 2 Kings 8:12, 13:7). Or, Hazael may have literally driven sledges over the bodies of Gilead's people.

1. The basic sin in Damascus' act was treating people barbarously, like things, in order to extract profit (1:3). How might a modern person treat people in similar ways?

___

___

___

___

Gaza (1:6). A Philistine commercial center. Businessmen in Gaza traded in many things, since the city was on a major route between Egypt, Palestine, and Assyria. Apparently, some men made a business of raiding villages in southern Judah and selling the people to neighboring Edom.

Ashdod . . . Ashkelon . . . Ekron (1:8). These were the other three major cities of Philistia.

2. a. What was Gaza's ultimate sinful act (1:6)?

___

___

___

___

b. Actual slave trading is rare in our day. Still, how might a modern person treat people with the same attitudes that led the men of Gaza to kidnap and sell people?

____

____

____

____

____

Study Skill—Application

If you are having trouble making analogies between the sins of the nations and sins modern people might commit, here is an example: *I sin like Damascus when I seek to attain some selfish goal by overrunning other people, shaking and tearing them to extract what I want as though they were a cash crop belonging to me. I do this in "small" ways to my family when I yell to make them do what I want. Some people do this in big ways to employees and business competitors.*

The key is to see the self-centered attitude behind each of the nations' sins.

Tyre (1:9). "The senior Phoenician merchant city, allied to Israel by a 'treaty of brotherhood' in the days of David (1 Kings 5:1), later in the time of Solomon (1 Kings 5:12), and later still during the reign of Ahab . . . (1 Kings 16:30-31)."[3]

3. a. Tyre was supposed to behave as a brother to Israel. What sinful attitude lies behind the act of selling one's brother for profit?

____

____

____

____

For Thought and Discussion: a. Why do you suppose the Lord began His indictment of Israel with judgments upon the nations around Israel, nations who had no covenant with Him and little knowledge of His Law and character? (*Optional:* See Romans 1:18-22, 2:6-15.)

b. What do you learn about the Lord's character from 1:3-2:3?

Optional Application: Does 1:3-2:3 remind you of anyone for whom you might pray, asking that God would move them to repentance and would treat their sins with mercy rather than judgment? Think of people you know, your nation, other nations. If you think of anyone, commit yourself to pray for them.

b. How might a modern person act similarly?

Edom (1:11). Traditionally kin to Israel, since Edom (Esau) and Israel (Jacob) were brothers (Genesis 25:23-26). Edom may have shared in the slave trade with Gaza and Tyre, but its ultimate sin concerned the endless wars between Israel and Edom (2 Kings 8:20-22).

---

4. How might a modern person treat a "brother" with attitudes like Edom's (1:11)?

Rabbah (1:14). This city is now called Amman, the capital of Jordan, but in Amos' day Rabbah was the capital of the nation Ammon.

---

5. What desire led the king of Ammon to lead a genocide on the people of Gilead, killing both present and future generations (1:13)?

Burned as if to lime (2:1). Moab and Edom had a long history of bitterness between them. Once, Edom wreaked slaughter and destruction across Moab, but Moab failed to kill Edom's king in battle. So, the Moabite king had the Edomite king's son captured and sacrificed on a city wall (2 Kings 3:26-27). Some years later, another Moabite king unearthed the remains of a dead Edomite king and had them burned to ash.

Cremation was not practiced in the ancient Near East, for people believed that a man's spirit could rest only if the body was decently buried.[4] Thus, as Ammon showed utter disrespect for persons yet unborn, so Moab deliberately desecrated a dead person. While Ammon's motive was greed for possessions and power, Moab's was hatred.

For Thought and Discussion: What can 1:3-2:3 teach us about Christ's mission and the reason for His death?

6. Can you think of any ways a person might sin like Ammon or Moab?

____

____

____

____

____

Study Skill—Summarizing the Passage

You will remember more of what you study if you summarize the main teaching of each passage. Consider these questions:

What is the Lord talking about in this passage?

What does this have to do with His overall message in the book?

Why does He say this here? (In this case, why does He begin the book with this topic?)

7. How would you summarize the message of 1:3-2:3?

____

For Further Study: Next to the names of the six pagan nations in the outline on page 18, write the sin that nation committed. Or, begin making your own outline of the book. Doing this will help you to remember what God is saying in this passage.

8. What principles about justice can we learn from this passage?

9. Does anything in 1:3-2:3 have implications for your life? (Consider the optional applications on pages 30 and 33.) If so, write down how you might respond to what you have studied.

10. List any questions you have about anything in this passage.

For the group

Read aloud. To get the full impact of this opening prophecy, read 1:3-2:3 aloud. You could have a different person read the judgment on each nation.

Summarize. In a way, the Lord is saying the same thing six times to six different nations in this passage. So before you look at each sin in detail, clarify the Lord's overall point. What is He talking about? What is the structure of each oracle? Why does He say all this before speaking about Judah and finally Israel in 2:4-16?

This last question requires some logical reasoning, not just wild speculation. Consider the message the Lord is getting across to Israel; consider how the people of Israel might have felt to hear these oracles. Don't get bogged down in this question, however. If you can't see a reason for this beginning now, you may see it later.

Six sins. Take as much time as you need to clarify who each of the six nations was, but remember that this is just background to understand the point the Lord is making. Instead, focus on 1) what each nation's sin was, 2) what attitudes toward people lay behind each sin, and 3) how a modern person might commit not necessarily the same sin, but a sin with the same attitude behind it.

Notice that the Lord did not judge the nations according to the Law of Moses, for they did not know it. Rather, He judged them by the basic standards of justice that all people recognized. If you like, look at Romans 1:18-22 and 2:6-15 in this context.

Your response. Ideally, you will be able to spend about half of your discussion time on application, since this is the most important part of the study. You can explore what Amos 1:3-2:3 says to people of our day in general and what it says to you personally.

Encourage group members to decide to make some specific response to the passage—confession, prayer, or action. If members are not well acquainted or if application is new to them, they may prefer not to expose their sins and intentions to the group, and the group should respect that preference. Also, no one should be made to feel that he

Optional Application: a. Think about the sins of the six nations, and the attitudes toward people (living, unborn, dead, brothers, friends, enemies) that lay behind those sins. Do you ever show any similar attitudes? If so, what do you do that is wrong?

b. Confess your sin to God, and ask Him to help you notice times during the next week when you are tempted to show this wrong attitude. Also, ask Him to enable you to choose to do and think as Christ would.

c. Look for a chance during the coming week to act in a manner opposite to the wrong attitude you have found in yourself. What might you do?

must identify with at least one of the six sins. God may be moving that person to pray for others instead. In this context, the leader might read beforehand 2 Chronicles 7:14 and 1 John 1:8-10.

Your study group offers you a chance to help each other. For instance, you can plan to share next week the results to date of your commitments to apply 1:3-2:3. At that time you can air frustrations, insights, and joys, and you can clear up any misconceptions about application.

If you have time, try to connect this passage to the New Testament. How can it help us understand why Christ came and did what He did?

Summarize. Draw your discussion to a focused close by having someone summarize what the Lord is saying in 1:3-2:3 and how you have decided this message applies to you.

Worship. Praise God for the character He reveals in this passage of Amos. Thank Him that in Jesus, His mercy triumphs over His will to treat sin with justice. Thank Him that He is able not only to forgive us for sins like these, but also to free us from the self-centeredness that leads to these sins. Ask Him to forgive and free you. Also, ask Him to forgive and free any other people or nations that He prompts you to pray for.

Justice and Righteousness, part one

The Bible teaches that doing justice means conforming to a standard, acting according to a rule. Through the prophet Isaiah the Lord said, "I will make justice the measuring line and righteousness the plumb line; hail will sweep away your refuge, the lie . . ." (Isaiah 28:17; compare Amos 7:7-9). Justice means giving to each person his own, what he is due, as Paul says, "Give everyone what you owe him: If you owe taxes, pay taxes; if revenue, then revenue; if respect, then respect; if honor, then honor" (Romans 13:7).

The standard by which we decide what we owe each person is the Law of God. Jesus reaffirmed the Ten Commandments (Exodus

(continued on page 35)

(continued from page 34)

20:1-17, Deuteronomy 5:6-21, Matthew 5:17-48) and the two Great Commandments (Mark 12:29-31) as God's standard of justice. We know that we can never live up to God's standard in our own strength (Romans 3:20, 7:22-23). But Jesus' death fulfills the penalty for our failures and so allows God to forgive us (Romans 3:21-26), and the Spirit of God transforms us so that more and more we are able to obey God's standard (Romans 8:1-12, Galatians 5:13-18).

(continued on page 68)

1. J. A. Motyer, *The Day of the Lion* (Downer's Grove, Illinois: InterVarsity Press, 1974), pages 39-47. (Hereafter referred to as "Motyer.")
2. *The NIV Study Bible*, pages 545,1348.
3. *The NIV Study Bible*, page 1349; Motyer, page 39.
4. Martin-Achard, pages 19-20; *The NIV Study Bible*, page 1349.

LESSON THREE

AMOS 2:4-16

God's People Also

The first six nations were Israel's pagan neighbors, scorned as the unholy who were not the Lord's chosen people. Amos' Israelite audience probably applauded oracles of judgment against them. Perhaps the applause was even louder when Amos turned to tar Judah with the same brush—Judah, Israel's sister nation and chief rival not only for dominance in the region, but also for claim to the Lord's covenant promises. How, then, might Amos' audience have reacted when he began to condemn Israel with the same poetic form he had used for the depraved pagans and the arch-rival?

Read 2:4-16, asking God to show you His message for Israel and how it applies to us today.

Judah (2:4-5)

The pagan nations were judged according to the laws of human conscience, but the Lord held Judah to a higher standard. "All who sin apart from the law will also perish apart from the law, and all who sin under the law will be judged by the law" (Romans 2:12).

Law (2:4). Or, "teaching" (Hebrew: *torah*). It referred to all that God had revealed about Himself and His relationship with His people. Specifically, everything in the five books of

For Thought and Discussion: Consider the inevitable results of sin that Judah experienced. Does the same thing happen to a modern person who rejects the Lord's revelation of Himself, ignores His moral laws, and pursues popular goals? Why or why not?

Optional Application: Do any "false gods" (2:4, NASB: "lies") tempt you away from the Lord's teaching? If so, what are they?

Moses—Genesis through Deuteronomy—was *torah*. *Torah* had a wider meaning than our English word "law," for it included God's acts of grace in creating mankind, redeeming His people from slavery, caring for them in the wilderness, and forgiving their sins during that time.

Decrees (2:4). "Statutes" in RSV and NASB. The root is "to engrave"[1]; decrees are those eternal truths and values that the Lord has engraved into His creation. As 1:3-2:3 shows, God's moral laws dictate the same inevitable cause-and-effect that His laws of physics dictate. It has been said, "If you step off a cliff, you do not break the law of gravity, you illustrate it."[2]

Study Skill—Paraphrasing
Paraphrasing, putting Scripture into your own words, helps you to think about what it means.

1. In your own words, explain how Judah had sinned (2:4).

____

____

____

____

____

Israel (2:6-16)

2. Hardly pausing for breath, Amos turned to condemn Israel in the same form in which he had condemned Israel's enemies. What point might he have been making by using the same structure as before? (*Optional:* See Romans 2:1, 3:9.)

____

____

____

Righteous (2:6). It was lawful to sell a person into servitude for six years if he was unable to pay a debt (Leviticus 25:39-43). One meaning of "righteous" is "one who is in the right in a lawsuit." So, the righteous may have been people either sold into slavery or just deprived of their land and livelihood through false lawsuits. Powerful men accused ordinary people of owing them money, and they won their suits either by bribing judges or by arguing more cleverly than the accused could.[3]

Needy (2:6). These may have been sold for small debts; "a pair of sandals" suggests a pledge for a small amount. God's Law commanded Israelites to give to needy people without demanding repayment (Deuteronomy 15:7-11), but "business was business" for some Israelites. See Amos 8:6.[4]

Poor . . . oppressed (2:7). ("Helpless" and "humble" in NASB.) People with little power or low social standing, who were therefore vulnerable to cheating, extortion, and exploitation by those with power. They included people with little money, as well as common laborers, clerks, the elderly, children, single women, and others.[5]

3. Describe some modern parallels for selling the righteous and needy, trampling the poor, and denying justice to the oppressed.

For Thought and Discussion: How did Israel's sins differ from those of the pagan nations (2:7-8)?

Father . . . altar (2:7-8). This may mean that men were using household servants as family prostitutes. Or, men may have been visiting Canaanite cult prostitutes as though they were having family outings.

The Canaanites had at least three deities connected with fertility: the god Baal (lord of sun and rain), the goddess Asherah (goddess of fertility in crops and herds), and the goddess Ashtoreth or Astarte (Baal's consort, goddess of the moon and monthly cycles). The Canaanites believed that if they had ritualized sexual relations by the altar of one of these deities, then the deity would imitate the act and so cause the crops or herds or women to be fertile. Men and women called "holy ones" (masculine: *qadesh*; feminine: *qedesha*) were kept at temples to perform ritual sex with male worshipers. The Bible forbids these cult prostitutes in Leviticus 19:29 and Deuteronomy 23:17.[6]

4. Why was the Lord's "holy name" profaned when Israelites visited "holy women" at Canaanite shrines or abused household servants?

____

____

____

____

____

Garments taken in pledge (2:8). In Israel, people normally borrowed for immediate needs only, not to finance business ventures or to buy houses. Because it was assumed that only someone in financial need would borrow, the Law prohibited lenders from charging interest on loans. They were not to profit from others' misfortune, but to regard loans as acts of charity (Deuteronomy 23:19-20).

A lender could expect the borrower to

repay the amount loaned. He could hold one of the borrower's possessions as collateral (a pledge) during the day to prevent him from using it to secure several loans. However, a lender could not take something indispensable as collateral (Deuteronomy 24:6), nor invade a man's house to receive the collateral (Deuteronomy 24:10-11), nor keep a man's cloak overnight (Deuteronomy 24:12-13), nor take a widow's cloak at all (Deuteronomy 24:17).[7]

Fines (2:8). These were paid as restitution for damages in lawsuits, probably either exorbitant or based on false charges.[8]

---

5. a. What attitudes about people and money do God's laws about loans reflect?

____

____

____

____

____

   b. What attitudes toward people and money did the Israelites show (Amos 2:6-8)?

____

____

____

____

____

When the Lord made His covenant with Israel, He did not just give Israel a list of laws to keep; He also promised to favor Israel in some special ways. In contrast with the covenant-breaking sins of 2:6-8, the Lord lists His acts of covenant faithfulness in 2:9-11.

6. For each act of grace that the Lord bestowed on Israel (2:9-11), write a similar blessing you have received.

Optional Application: a. List as many gracious things the Lord has done for you as you can think of. Ponder this list for a while, and thank Him for His graciousness.

b. How are you responding to the Lord's generosity? How should you respond?

a. He delivered Israel's forefathers from oppression and gave them their own land and liberty to use it (2:9-10).

____

____

____

____

b. He gave Israel prophets, men who knew Him well and could proclaim His instruction (2:11).

____

____

____

____

c. He gave Israel Nazirites, men who modeled for the people lives of exceptional devotion to the Lord (2:11).

____

____

____

____

Nazirites (2:11-12). These men took "a vow of separation to the Lord" (Numbers 6:2) for a time or permanently. One aspect of their special holiness was abstention from fermented drinks and even from grapes, raisins, and grape seeds. "They had no special office" such as prophet or priest, but simply lived as "an evidence of what all might be and do if they used the grace of God."[9] See Numbers 6:1-8.

7. In response to the Lord's acts of grace, Israel corrupted the Nazirites, God's witnesses, and silenced the prophets, God's spokesmen (2:12).

How might professing Christians do something similar?

8. What was the promised consequence for rejecting God's laws and His acts of grace (2:13-16)?

9. Summarize the attitudes that the Lord expected of His people, according to 2:4-16.

social values (verses 6-8)

religious behavior (verses 4,7b-8)

response to the Lord's acts of covenant grace (verses 9-12)

For Further Study: Verses 14-16 list several things people might have been tempted to trust to save them from the Lord's judgment. What were those things?

For Further Study: Compare the attitudes you summarized in question 9 to the Ten Commandments (Exodus 20:1-17) or to Jesus' summary of the Law (Mark 12:28-31).

For Further Study: If no answer for question 11 comes to mind, try listing as many principles as you can find in 2:4-16 that are applicable to Christians today.

10. Now summarize the main point of 2:6-16 in a sentence.

____

____

____

____

____

____

Study Skill—Outlining

If you wanted to expand the outline on page 18 to remind yourself of what you have learned, you could break 2:4-16 up as follows. Try filling in titles for each of the subsections of 2:6-16.

2:4-6 Judah judged for abandoning God's covenant

2:6-16 Israel judged for abandoning God's covenant

2:6-8 ______________________________

____

2:9-11 ______________________________

____

2:12 ________________________________

____

2:13-16 _____________________________

____

Your response

11. a. Do you find any principles in 2:4-16 that apply to your life? If so, what value, attitude, or principle would you most like to put more fully into practice?

b. What steps could you take during the coming week to act on this principle or to adopt this attitude more fully?

12. Write down any questions you have about 2:4-16.

For the group

Worship.

Read aloud.

Summarize. As usual, try to grasp the Lord's overall point before you dive into the details of the passage. Can the group now think of any reasons why the book opens with six similar oracles against the nations, then gives one against Judah in the same form, and finally uses the same form for an oracle against Israel?

Optional Application: a. How can you help the *needy* in your community?

b. Seek out someone or some group in your community who is being *treated unjustly* by more powerful people. How can you find out what needs to happen for these oppressed ones to receive their due? How can you help them receive what they deserve? Before you make great plans, begin with prayer.

Sin and judgment. There is a lot of historical background material in this lesson, but the lesson's basic structure is fairly simple:

What were Judah's sins (question 1)?
What were Israel's sins (questions 3-7)?
What consequence did the Lord promise (question 8)?
What is the point of the passage (questions 2, 10)?
How is the passage relevant to our lives (questions 3, 9, 11)?

Without shortchanging time to clarify what Amos means by what he says, try to move toward how his words are relevant for us. Explore one or more of these angles:

What can we learn about the changeless character of God, and how should that affect how we act?
What principles of justice can we learn from this passage, and how can we apply them in our personal lives?
How are these principles of justice relevant to our actions as members of a community, a church, a nation, or the world?

You could respond to God's hatred of injustice as a group by:

praying together for guidance about what problems need to be addressed, and about how you might address them;
praying for people who are needy or oppressed;
sharing ideas;
sharing sources of information;
encouraging each other when attempts are frustrated;
approaching one problem as a group.

Old Testament Prophets, part two

After the Exodus from Egypt, the Lord made a treaty, or *covenant*, with Israel like a treaty between an overlord and a subject people. The people had agreed to serve and obey the Lord

(continued on page 47)

(continued from page 46)

as God, and to accept the consequences of obedience and disobedience. The agreed consequences of obedience were blessings (Deuteronomy 4:32-40, 28:1-14), and the agreed consequences of disobedience were punishments (Deuteronomy 28:15-68).

Because the Lord was patiently training His people as a father trains his children, He did not simply let the consequences fall on each generation. Instead, He sent prophets in each generation to tell how He thought the people were living up to the covenant, and how He planned to respond. When Israel was disobedient, the Lord sent prophets like Amos to warn that the agreed results were going to occur unless the people repented.

In this way, the people could never accuse the Lord of injustice. They had agreed to the standards of conduct and to the consequences, and the Lord never acted without ample forewarning and second chances.

(continued on page 106)

1. Motyer, page 55.
2. John and Paula Sandford, *The Transformation of the Inner Man* (Plainfield, New Jersey: Bridge Publishing Company, 1981), page 75.
3. *The NIV Study Bible*, page 1349; Motyer, page 56; Mays, page 46.
4. Motyer, page 56; Martin-Achard, page 21; *The NIV Study Bible*, page 1350.
5. Motyer, page 57; Martin-Achard, page 21; Mays, page 46.
6. Motyer, pages 57-59.
7. Roland de Vaux, *Ancient Israel: Volume 1: Social Institutions* (New York: McGraw-Hill Book Company, 1965), page 78; J. A. Thompson, *Deuteronomy: An Introduction and Commentary (London: Inter-Varsity Press, 1974), page 242; Peter C. Craigie, The Book of Deuteronomy* (Grand Rapids, Michigan: William B. Eerdmans Publishing Company, 1976), page 302.
8. *The NIV Study Bible*, page 1350.
9. E. B. Pusey, *The Minor Prophets, II: Amos* (Grand Rapids, Michigan: Baker Book House, [1906]); see Motyer, page 62.

LESSON FOUR

AMOS 3:1-15

The Chosen Judged

Amos begins a new section in 3:1. "Hear this word" he says in 3:1, 4:1, and 5:1, each time proceeding to indict Israel for its sins. "Therefore" he says in 3:11, 4:12, and 5:16, each time stating the consequences of those sins.

Read 3:1-15, asking the Sovereign Lord to show you Himself through these words.

The lion has roared (3:1-8)

Besides forming the beginning of a new section, 3:1-8 also rounds out the first section of Amos' prophecy. He began in 1:2, saying "The LORD roars"; he looks back in 3:8, saying "The lion has roared."[1] What gives Amos the right to announce the outrageous prophecy of 1:2-2:16 to God's chosen, beloved people? In 3:1-8, Amos explains.

Study Skill—Connecting Words

Connecting words show how one idea relates to another. "Therefore" in 3:2 points to the result of a cause. Watch for other connectives, such as:

when (time);
because, for, since (reason);
in order that, so that (purpose);
although, but, yet (contrast);
also, likewise, just as . . . so (comparison).

For Thought and Discussion: a. What does it mean for Christians that we are now God's chosen people (1 Peter 2:9-10)? What privileges and responsibilities does this status include?

b. Why does God have a special right to judge His chosen people? See Hebrews 12:4-11, 1 Peter 4:17.

Optional Application: Does 3:2 have any implications for your attitudes and behavior? Consider memorizing this verse and taking some extended time to think about it.

Chosen (3:2). Literally, "known." It implies intimacy, fellowship, love (see Genesis 4:1). In Psalm 1:6, "knows" means "watches over" to protect.

---

1. God had chosen Israel for a unique status and relationship with Him (3:2), and He had shown His love by saving Israel from slavery in Egypt (3:1). But Israel thought election meant only privilege, protection, and intimacy.

   a. Explain the "therefore" in 3:2. What does election mean besides intimacy?

   ____

   ____

   ____

   ____

   b. In what ways can Christians today take their relationship with God for granted as Israel did?

   ____

   ____

   ____

   ____

   ____

   ____

2. a. Amos' point in 3:3 is that the Lord and Israel walk together because they have a covenant agreement to walk together. But if one party rejects the agreed path, while the other party remains faithful to the agreed path, what happens?

   ____

   ____

   ____

b. What implications, if any, does this principle have for the Christian life?

3. In 3:4-6, Amos builds a series of rhetorical questions to explain his statement in 3:2. Think about these pictures of cause and effect.

a. The roaring lion, the snap of the trap, and the trumpet blown in a city are all sounds that inform or warn the listener of something. What warning of looming disaster has Israel received (1:2, 3:7-8)?

b. The prey is caught because a lion does it; the bird is caught because a trap does it; and—finally—a city is caught because the Lord does it. Therefore, if calamity befalls a sinful nation, what should the people and later generations conclude (3:6)?

4. In 3:7-8, Amos gives us some insight into the prophetic office. Describe the relationship between the Lord and His prophet implied in 3:7.

Optional Application: Examine your life in light of 3:3. Is your intimacy with God suffering because you are disagreeing about the path or the pace of your walk together? If so, what can you do about this?

For Thought and Discussion: Has the Lord given any warning signs in your day? If so, what are they, and what should Christians do?

For Further Study: Did God reject His chosen people (3:2)? Some passages to study carefully are Matthew 3:7-10, 7:21-22, 22:1-14; Romans 9:6-8, 10:16, 11:2, 11:25-29 (or all of Romans 9-11).

For Thought and Discussion: Why do you suppose "the Sovereign LORD does nothing without revealing his plan to his servants the prophets" (3:7)? Consider question 3 above, and the boxes on pages 25 and 46.

For Further Study: Prophecy was an office in the New Testament Church also. Look at Acts 11:27-29, 21:10-14; 1 Corinthians 14:3-4. What function did prophets have in the early Church?

For Thought and Discussion: What does 3:1-8 show you about the Lord's character? How does He reflect the same character in our day?

5. What is the prophet's motive for speaking (3:8)?

6. Summarize Amos' point in 3:1-8. Consider how it fits into the total message of the book.

Covenant lawsuit (3:9-15)

Study Skill—Prophetic Forms, part one

There are several standard forms in which the prophets would often state their messages. One form is the *lawsuit*, which portrays the Lord as a sovereign bringing suit against a subject for breaking a covenant/treaty. "The full lawsuit contains a summons, a charge, evidence, and a verdict, though these elements may sometimes be implied rather than explicit."[2]

(continued on page 53)

For Thought and Discussion: Read Romans 2:23-25. Why would the Lord choose pagans as witnesses against Israel?

(continued from page 52)

Amos 3 shows elements of the lawsuit form. "Hear this word" (3:1) begins the formal charge. In 3:9 the Lord calls the fortresses of Ashdod and Egypt as witnesses against Israel, and in 3:13 He calls the witnesses to testify. "Therefore" in 3:11 begins the sentence after an implied verdict of guilty. Watch for this form in other prophecies, such as Isaiah 3.

(continued on page 71)

In 1:2-2:16, Amos announced the Lord's judgment upon many nations, and above all on Israel. In 3:1-8, he proved his right and his compulsion to proclaim this judgment. Now, in 3:9-6:14 Amos vindicates the Lord's justice—he details the sins that make Israel worthy of destruction. We should envision a sovereign proving his case against a rebellious subject, so that all his subjects will acknowledge his justice.

Ashdod (3:9). RSV and other versions read "Assyria" following the Septuagint (the Greek translation of the Old Testament). However, the Hebrew text of Amos names the Philistine city, Ashdod (see on 1:8). According to the Hebrew text, Amos never named Assyria, but only hinted at the tool of the Lord's judgment.

Philistia and Egypt were old enemies of Israel. Egypt had held the Israelites in slavery for four centuries until the Lord delivered them miraculously. After that, Israel had periodically wrestled against Egyptian attempts to control the profitable trade routes from Egypt to Assyria. The Philistines had arrived on the coast of Palestine about the time the Israelites had arrived from Egypt, and the two groups had been fighting over land and control of trade ever since (see the books of Joshua, Judges, and 1 Samuel).

To Israel, the Philistines and Egyptians were the extreme of uncircumcised, godless pagans. It was a slap in the face for the Lord to call them as witnesses, as though they were Israel's peers or superiors.

For Thought and Discussion: a. Think about the unrest, or tumults, within the Samaritan fortresses (3:9). Why do you think the people were in conflict with each other? See Philippians 2:3-4, James 4:1-3.

b. What makes people not know how to do right (3:10)? See Ephesians 4:18.

Fortresses (3:9-11). "Citadels" in NASB; "strongholds" in RSV; "palaces" in KJV. The dwellings of the powerful were luxurious inside (3:12,15) and fortifed with thick walls and soldiers outside. The Lord calls the fortresses of the pagans to witness against the Israelite aristocrats, walled up in their fortresses.

---

7. In your own words, explain what the Lord saw going on inside the Samaritan fortresses (3:9-10).

unrest (RSV, NASB: "tumults") ______

oppression ______

not knowing how to do right ______

hoarding plunder and loot (RSV: "violence and robbery")

As a shepherd . . . (3:12). A shepherd could seldom save a lamb's life if a lion caught it, but he did try to save some pieces to prove to the owner that he had not stolen the lamb.

The Israelites believe that the Lord will always save them from enemies as He saved their ancestors from Egypt. He is their powerful and loving Shepherd. However, the Lord declares ironically that now He is the devouring Lion, and only a few bits of Israel will be saved from His wrath.

Altars of Bethel (3:14). The shrine that Jeroboam I set up to rival the Temple at Jerusalem. He wanted a religion that would never challenge his government, and the people were glad to be free to worship as they pleased.

Horns of the altar (3:14). It was a Near Eastern tradition that a criminal was immune as long as he clung to the horns at the corners of an altar. However, the Lord had said that deliberate murderers were not immune from punishment (Exodus 21:12-14; 1 Kings 1:49-53, 2:28-34).

8. Summarize 3:1-15:

the reasons for judgment ____________________

____

____

____

____

therefore . . .

the description of judgment ____________________

____

____

____

____

For Thought and Discussion: Does 3:12 suggest that the Lord intended to abandon His covenant with Israel and completely destroy the nation, or that He had not utterly rejected His chosen people? Why or why not? (See Amos 7:1-9, 9:9-15; Romans 9:1-11:36.)

For Thought and Discussion: a. Why was it sinful to seek refuge from guilt at the horns of the altar at Bethel?

b. The Israelites believed wrongly that God would save them from punishment if they clung to those horns. How might a modern person make a similar mistake?

Optional Application: Respond in prayer to what you learn from 3:1-15 about the Lord and how He deals with His people. Praise Him for His character and actions.

For Thought and Discussion: In what sorts of fortresses do modern people hoard their possessions? What should they do instead, according to Amos?

9. How does 3:1-15 fit into the overall theme of Amos' message?

Your response

10. Review the sins Amos discusses in 3:9-14. Below, list at least three questions modern Christians should ask themselves to see if these sins apply to them.

a. Am I contributing to "unrest" in my family, church, work-place, community? If so, how? What can I do about this?

b.

c.

d.

11. a. Is God saying anything to you through this chapter of Amos? If so, what seems to apply to you?

b. What prayer, action, or reassessment of your life might you pursue this week in light of this word from the Lord?

Study Skill—Application

In Amos' day, a person who became conscious of sin brought a sin offering for the priest to sacrifice. The person confessed his sin, and the animal suffered his penalty for him (Leviticus 4:1-5:13). When a Christian sins, he confesses his sin to God and asks Him to accept Jesus' death in place of his own. This substitution removes guilt.

Once free from guilt, the Israelite had little power to resist the habit of sin. The Christian, however, has the Spirit of God inside him, transforming his nature and empowering

(continued on page 58)

(continued from page 57)

him to resist sin. The Christian must simply choose to "walk" as the Spirit leads (Amos 3:3, Galatians 5:16) and use the power He provides (Romans 8:12-13). The New Testament has much to say about how to yield to the Spirit, but one clue is to focus on the character of God—the Father, Jesus, and the Spirit.

The book of Amos is good for meditating on God's character. Try to see how the ferocity shown in these early chapters is consistent with the character portrayed in Luke 13:34-35, 15:11-32; John 3:16-21; 1 John 3:16-18. If Amos' view of God seems hard, look for the balancing view in later passages.

12. List any questions you have about chapter 3.

____

____

____

____

For the group

Summarize. Ask someone to summarize 3:1-8 and someone else to summarize 3:9-15. Then have someone summarize the whole chapter. Let other group members correct or add to the summaries, but don't spend a lot of time on this now. Initial summaries should be sound enough to give you a basis for discussing individual verses, but they need not be the last word on the subject since you will summarize again at the end of your discussion.

Chosen. Chosenness is a key concept in this chapter. You might look at how different versions translate 3:2—"You only have I known . . . ," "You only have I chosen . . . ," "You only have Me . . . ." What does it mean to be known or chosen by someone? In what sense was Israel known or chosen by God? What responsibilities and privileges went along with that status? In what sense are Christians known or chosen by God? What responsibilities and privileges go along with that status? Does Amos 3:2 apply to Christians in any ways? How, or why not?

Question 1 tries to explore what 3:2 means and how it applies to us, question 2 does the same with 3:3, and question 3 does the same with 3:4-6. If anything about a question is unclear, you can always rephrase: "What is Amos' point in verse(s) . . . ?" "How does this apply to us?" Give group members a chance to ask questions about anything that remains unclear.

The prophetic office. Questions 4 and 5 examine what an Old Testament prophet was and did. See also the boxes on pages 25, 46, 99, and 106.

Lawsuit. When a passage contains allusions that may be unfamiliar to group members, it is often a good idea to ask questions about the explanatory material in the study guide. For instance, you might ask, "What did Israel think of Egypt? How did Israel regard Ashdod? What did Amos mean by calling the fortresses of those nations to witness against Israel?" Of course, you won't want to discuss mostly background and ignore the point of what the Lord is saying (questions 7-9) and what that has to do with you (questions 10-11).

The optional questions in the margins offer some specific avenues of application; however, your group may have other avenues in mind.

Discuss the character of God that is revealed in Amos 1-3. It's easy to see Him as the fierce Old Testament Lion, totally different from the merciful, self-giving New Testament Lamb. However, how did He show grace (2:9-11, 3:1-2) and patience (3:7) toward Israel? How did he show loving concern for people (1:3,6,9,13; 2:1,6-8; 3:9-10)? As for His mercy, consider why Jesus' death was necessary.

Summarize.

Worship. Praise God for the character He has revealed to you. Thank Him for choosing you, for knowing you, with all the privileges and responsibilities that includes. Thank Him for showing you the behavior He expects and the just consequences of rebellion. Above all, thank Him for sending Jesus to bear the just consequences of your rebellion, and for sending His Spirit to enable you to abandon self-centeredness.

Names of God

We can learn a great deal about a prophet's subtle message from noticing how he refers to God. For example, Amos seldom calls Him "the God of Israel." When we also observe that Amos never uses the word "covenant" but does refer to the responsibilities of being God's chosen ones (2:9-11, 3:2), we can suspect that Amos was trying not to encourage Israel's complacency. Instead, Amos calls God:

1. *the LORD* (His covenant name, YHWH. See page 20.);
2. *the Sovereign LORD* (NASB, RSV: "the Lord GOD");
3. *the Lord* (meaning "the Sovereign," "the Ruler");
4. *the LORD God Almighty* (NASB, RSV: "the LORD God of hosts." This means that He is Lord over the powers of heaven and the armies of Israel; He is omnipotent.);
5. Compound titles, as in 5:16.

All these titles emphasize God's universal rule. Amos further stresses this point by showing in 1:3-2:3 that the Lord is judge over all the nations, not just Israel.

But there is more. Not only is God "the LORD"—the covenant God who "brought you up out of Egypt" (2:10, 3:1-2)—He is also "the LORD *your* God" (4:12, 9:15). In the midst of judgment, the covenant relationship is unbroken.[3]

1. Motyer, page 33.
2. Fee and Stuart, page 160.
3. J. A. Motyer, "Amos," *The New Bible Commentary: Revised* (Grand Rapids, Michigan: William B. Eerdmans Publishing Company, 1970), pages 726-727. (This work is not cited again.)

LESSON FIVE

AMOS 4:1-13

Prepare to Meet Your God

In chapter 3, the Lord began to explain why He was roaring, and why He was going to send an "enemy" to "overrun the land" (3:11). Chapter 4 continues this theme.

Read through the chapter, making mental note of each of Israel's sins. Even more importantly, look for the character and attributes the Lord reveals in His words to His rebellious chosen ones.

For Thought and Discussion: Why do you suppose Amos compared the rich women to choice cattle?

For Further Study: Compare the description in Amos 4:1 to the portrait of a godly woman in Proverbs 31.

For Thought and Discussion: Was the Lord opposed to wealth? What attitude toward wealth did He expect of Israel? Support your responses with Scripture.

Unrepentance (4:1-11)

Bashan (4:1). A region of Israel just east of the Jordan River and the Sea of Galilee. (See the map on page 9.) It was renowned for its choice, pampered cattle.

1. What was wrong with the way the rich women of Samaria treated their husbands and their subordinates (4:1)?

____

____

____

____

____

For Thought and Discussion: a. If the Lord was angry about how the people were acquiring and using their money, why was He not satisfied by tithing? What did He want the people to do instead?

b. What implications do the Lord's words have for the ways we acquire and use money?

c. What else does 4:1,4-5 show was wrong with the people's behavior and attitudes? (See the paragraph labeled "Unrepentance" on page 68.)

For Thought and Discussion: a. Amos never mentions sin offerings and confession as part of Israel's worship. What is wrong with religion that is full of thank offerings without confession, repentance, and atonement for sin?

b. What would be wrong with religion full of confession without thanks and praise?

Bethel . . . Gilgal (4:4). Shrines in Israel, popular because of their connection with Israel's glorious past as the Lord's favored nation. Chapter 5 (lesson six) has more to say about them.

Sacrifices (4:4). The Law required the nation to burn sacrifices every morning (Exodus 29:38-42).

Tithes every three years (4:4). Literally, "days," as in most other versions. Individuals were supposed to bring a special tithe every three years (Deuteronomy 14:28). NIV interprets that Amos is using "day" as a Hebrew idiom for "year." Alternatively, he may be sarcastically saying that the people can tithe 360 extra times and the Lord will not be impressed.

Leavened bread (4:5). Only unleavened bread was burned in sacrifice, for leaven symbolized impurity, and the Lord could receive only pure, holy things (Leviticus 2:11).

Thank offering . . . freewill offerings (4:5). "Thank offerings were given in gratitude for deliverance from sickness . . . , trouble . . . , or death . . . , or for a blessing received."[1] A freewill offering was supposed to be a gesture of love, preferably done privately.

---

2. Think about the people's attitudes and motives in worship (4:5). From this verse, can you tell why the Lord rejected the tithes and offerings Israel brought to Him? (*Optional:* See Matthew 6:1-4, Luke 11:42, 12:1.)

____

____

____

____

____

____

3. How might a modern Christian commit sins like those in 4:1 or 4:4-5?

____

____

____

____

____

____

Hooks (4:2). "Prisoners of war were led away with a rope fastened to a hook that pierced the nose or lower lip."[2] This was humiliating and excruciatingly painful.

4. While the people had been enjoying themselves with self-indulgent consumption (4:1) and religion (4:4-5), what had the Lord been doing (4:6-11)?

____

____

____

____

5. Why did He do this? (Think about what the word "returned" in 4:6-11 means.)

____

____

____

____

____

6. The disasters of 4:6-11 were so bad that Israel survived not because of the nation's strength,

For Thought and Discussion: People interpret tragedies in various ways. To some, they are always chance events of a random world. To others, they always result from the sin of the sufferer. To still others, they result sometimes from the sufferer's sin and sometimes from the sins of countless people in a corrupt world. Can you think of any principles for understanding tragedies? (You might see Amos 4:6-11, Luke 13:1-5, John 9:1-3, Romans 8:18-21, Hebrews 12:2-13, 1 Peter 4:12-19.)

For Thought and Discussion: Name some possible reasons why the people failed to repent when so much ill befell them.

but only "like a burning stick snatched from a fire" (4:11). How does this image reveal God's grace? (*Optional:* See Isaiah 1:9.)

Patience ended (4:12-13)

Since Israel had not taken the Lord's subtle and not-so-subtle hints, the Lord would resort to outright confrontation.

7. a. What might it mean to "meet" God in this context?

   b. How do you think the Lord wanted His people to prepare to meet Him (4:12)?

   c. What does this plea tell you about His attitude toward them?

8. Tell what you learn about God from each of the following passages. (Skip any that tell you nothing.)

"the Sovereign LORD . . . his holiness" (4:2)

"I gave you . . . yet you have not returned" (4:6)

"You were like a burning stick [that I] snatched from the fire" (4:11)

"prepare to meet your God" (4:12)

Optional Application: Do you need to do anything to "prepare to meet your God"? If so, what? Ponder this verse.

Optional Application: Meditate on the Lord's nature as revealed in 4:13. How should perceiving His nature affect your life?

Optional Application: Amos well depicts God's sovereignty. According to Romans 8:31-39, why is His sovereignty joyous as well as fearful for Christians? How might you respond this week to the Lord's sovereignty?

For Further Study: Try outlining chapter 4 by giving titles to 4:1-3, 4:4-5, and 4:6-11. You can add this chapter outline to a book outline like the one on page 18.

"He who forms . . . creates . . . reveals . . . turns . . . and treads . . .—the LORD God Almighty is his name." (4:13)

9. Summarize 4:1-13:

reasons for confrontation

therefore

Your response

10. What implications does 4:1-13 have for your life this week? How can you respond to what you have learned about the Lord?

11. Write down any questions you have about chapter 4.

For the group

Actions and attitudes. There are two kinds of reasons why the women in 4:1 are condemned and the worship in 4:4-5 is rejected. The *actions* done or not done are wrong, and so are the *attitudes* behind the people's actions. In questions 1 and 2, try to list what the people were doing that they should not have been doing (acquiring money by exploiting poorer workers . . .), what they were not doing that they should have been doing (helping the poor to become better able to provide for themselves . . .), and what attitudes they should have had about themselves, each other, the Lord, their money, offerings, and so on. Then see how this list applies to the ways we think about and act toward people, things, and the Lord (question 3).

One danger of this kind of discussion is that people may read their own political views into Amos' message. This is especially easy when people know little about the social/political/economic structure that actually existed in Israel and little about the system that God's Law actually taught. We need to be very cautious when we try to use the Old Testament to defend policies regarding state-run welfare, state-ownership socialism, commune-ownership socialism, or industrial free-market capitalism.

Perhaps a better approach would be to ask what we as individuals and groups can do about unjust actions and unrighteous attitudes in ourselves and our society—without resorting to unjust means like coercion and unrighteous attitudes like condemnation and bitterness.

Unrepentance. Questions 4-6 deal with how the Lord tried to use disasters in people's lives. Look for signs of His character in 4:6-11. Why was it just for Him to use disasters? What was His goal? What signs of mercy, love, and patience do you see? Why did He decide to stop being patient?

Patience ended. Question 7 explores the meaning of a key verse in this passage, one which has many subtle meanings. "Meeting" God can be terrifying, humbling, destroying, and transforming depending on the attitude with which a person meets Him. Take a little time to consider the character of God (question 8 takes an overview of this aspect of the chapter), and then explore the various connotations of meeting God.

Try to give everyone a chance to share how the chapter moves him or her to respond. Then summarize the chapter and your discussion.

Worship. Focusing on the character of God leads naturally to worship. As you praise Him for His nature, ask Him to show you how to prepare to meet Him. Confess any wrong attitudes and habits that seem difficult to let go of.

Justice and Righteousness, part two

Justice has to do with behavior. The Bible speaks of *just transactions*, in which neither force nor fraud interferes with the free exchange of goods and services. It calls for *impartial judges* to decide guilt or innocence and to set fair punishment or compensation in civil or criminal disputes; the judge must apply the law's standard to discern what each party is due. Finally, the Bible gives guidance on how to *divide goods and tasks* among people.

In each case the standard is *justice*, not necessarily *equality*. We do not necessarily owe

(continued on page 69)

(continued from page 68)
each person the same amount of our time, the same wage, the same lifestyle, reward, or punishment. Rather, we owe him his due in proportion to the situation: time in proportion to our intimacy with him and his need; wage in proportion to his task; punishment in proportion to his crime. Justice demands equal standards for all people, not equal results. Different abilities, morals, interests, and so on will lead people to different places.[3]

Justice is the Bible's standard for governments, public affairs, and business. However, God's Law calls private individuals to a higher standard when dealing with other individuals: "You shall love your neighbor as yourself" (Leviticus 19:18, Luke 10:25-37, Romans 13:8-10). Passages like Deuteronomy 10:18-19; 15:1-11; 22:1-3; 23:19-20; 24:10-13,19-22 all command people to go beyond strict justice to love their neighbors because God is loving as well as just. For the government, the standard is justice for all; for the individual, the standard is selfless love for all.

(continued on page 81)

1. *The NIV Study Bible*, page 154.
2. *The NIV Study Bible*, page 1352; see also Mays, pages 72-73.
3. Ronald Nash, *Social Justice and the Christian Church* (Milford, Michigan: Mott Media, 1983), pages 27-38; Peter A. De Vos, "Justice," *Baker's Dictionary of Christian Ethics*, edited by Carl F. Henry (Grand Rapids, Michigan: Baker Book House, 1973), pages 360-362.

LESSON SIX

AMOS 5:1-27

Seek Me

Study Skill—Prophetic Forms, part two

In chapter 5, Amos uses two more forms that the prophets used frequently.

Verse 2 has the traditional rhythm of a Hebrew *lament*, the customary dirge that mourners would sing at funerals. Professional mourners were often hired to weep and wail loudly as a body was carried to burial. The motif of wailing mourners appears again in 5:16.

Verse 18 begins a related form, the *woe oracle*. "Woe" was a word normally used to express grief at a funeral or when some disaster had occurred. "Alas" (NASB) is another good translation of this word, which communicates sorrow, heartfelt anguish, rather than anger. The typical woe oracle begins with an announcement of "woe" (5:18), then gives the reason for the distress (5:18-26), and ends with a prediction of doom (5:27).[1] Observe the same pattern in chapter 6.

(continued on page 112)

For the Lord and for Amos, the destruction of Israel was not an occasion for vindictive celebration. Rather, it was an occasion for grief and mourning as they felt the anguish the Israelites would suffer because of folly.

Read 5:1-27, looking for the theme and the emotion in this speech.

1. Verses 4-5 summarize the appeal of 5:4-27. The message is . . .

   do ______________________________

   ____

   do not ______________________________

   ____

   because ______________________________

   ____

Chapter 5 is a carefully constructed sermon, but many of its allusions are lost on us because we know little about Israel's religious traditions. Into the framework of a mourning song, Amos weaves an appeal based on three popular Israelite holy places: Bethel, Beersheba, and Gilgal (5:5). Each shrine had vivid connotations for Israel—Bethel symbolized the transformation of Jacob into Israel; Beersheba reminded that God was present with His people, and Gilgal signified that God had "rolled" away the shame of slavery. Amos used these three symbols of Israel's pride to condemn the nation.[2]

Transformation (5:6-13)

The ancient shrine at Bethel was associated with Jacob, who first arrived there as a young man fleeing his brother Esau's wrath (Genesis 28:10-22). Jacob had cheated Esau of his inheritance, but now Jacob was out alone to fend for himself, with only the vaguest idea of what to do.

One night as Jacob camped alone, the Lord revealed Himself in a dream. He gave Jacob the promises of land and descendants that He had given Abraham and Isaac. In response, the awed young man committed himself personally to worship and obey his fathers' God; thus the covenant was sealed with the third generation. Jacob called his campsite Bethel ("house of God") because, he said, "Surely the LORD is in this place" (Genesis 28:16).

Jacob then went to his uncle Laban and kept sheep for him for twenty years. Jacob married two wives, fathered twelve children, and collected large herds, but his cleverness also gained him his uncle's suspicion and his cousins' envy. Again Jacob fled, after the Lord appeared in a dream and called him back to Bethel. On the way, Jacob stopped at Peniel, where he wrestled with God. There the Lord changed his name from Jacob ("he supplants") to Israel ("he struggles with God"). The next day, Jacob met Esau and was reconciled to him. But instead of going on to Bethel, Jacob took a side trip to Shechem which ended in disaster. At last Jacob was ready to obey the Lord and return to Bethel.

The Lord had kept His promises to care for Jacob, and now Jacob made his household abandon their other gods and purify themselves. He built an altar to the Lord at Bethel, and the Lord appeared again and reaffirmed His promises. As a sign that Jacob was becoming a new person as he deepened his commitment to the Lord, the Lord again bestowed on him the new name, Israel. From then on, Jacob-Israel remained loyal.

Thus, Bethel was symbolically the place where God transformed the scheming, wayward Jacob into the obedient Israel, father of the nation. At this shrine, Israelites celebrated their inheritance of God's promises to Jacob-Israel.

2. Bethel meant transformation. But what kind of transformations did the Israelites practice (5:7)?

____

____

____

The Pleides and Orion (5:8). These constellations begin to appear in the sky in the fall and disappear in spring. Therefore, they were used to mark the change of the seasons.[3]

3. Israelites went to Bethel to seek the God who transformed Jacob into a nation. Amos sings a

For Thought and Discussion: Did the Bethel worshipers have the right to claim the blessings and promises Jacob received at Bethel? Why or why not?

For Thought and Discussion: What kind of transformation does the Lord promise to someone who seeks Him (5:4)?

For Thought and Discussion: If Israel failed to "seek the LORD", how did He promise to transform the nation (5:1-3,6)?

hymn of His transforming power in 5:8-9. What does he say about God?

4. From 5:10-13, does it seem that the Israelites were transformed as Jacob was by seeking the Lord at Bethel? Why or why not?

5. Instead of seeking Him at Bethel, the Lord urges the people to "Seek me and live" (5:4). What do you think He means by "Seek me"?

6. State in one sentence the promise and responsibility of Bethel, 5:6-13.

If you ______

then ______

but if you ______________________________

____

then ______________________________

____

Optional Application:
a. Meditate on the command, "Seek me and live" frequently over the next few days. How could you seek the Lord more fully?

b. Meditate on the description of the Lord in 5:8-9. What difference might seeking this God make to your priorities?

God with us (5:14-17)

King Abimelech made a covenant of friendship with Abraham at Beersheba and acknowledged the well there as Abraham's property. Abimelech said of Abraham, "God is with you in everything you do" (Genesis 21:22). When Isaac sojourned at Beersheba years later, "the LORD appeared to him and said, 'I am the God of your father Abraham. Do not be afraid, for I am with you . . .'" (Genesis 26:24). Abimelech recognized the same truth about Isaac as about Abraham (Genesis 26:28). Finally, Jacob passed through Beersheba on his way to join Joseph in Egypt. There God said in a vision, "I am God, the God of your father. . . . Do not be afraid to go down to Egypt, for I will make you into a great nation there. I will go down to Egypt with you . . ." (Genesis 46:3-4).

Thus, worshipers at Beersheba celebrated the knowledge that the Lord had promised to be present with their ancestors. The worshipers believed that God was with them, too, because of their ancestors' faithfulness and because they visited the shrines regularly. After all, wasn't Israel's prosperity proof that God was with His people?

7. However, what did the Lord expect the people to do so that He could be with them (5:14-15)?

____

____

____

____

____

8. If they failed to do this, how would He be with them, in their midst (5:16-17)?

Optional Application: How can you actively seek good among the people with whom you come in contact? How can you actively help to establish justice in your local and national courts? What sorts of help might you need to do these things?

For Thought and Discussion: Is it wrong for us to long for the day of the Lord? What attitudes should we have about that day?

____

____

____

____

Let justice roll (5:18-27)

Gilgal had been an important center of worship since the Israelites entered the promised land. As soon as they crossed the Jordan River, Joshua piled twelve stones from the river at Gilgal as a memorial of how God had dried up the Jordan for them to cross. The pile was a symbol of God actively fulfilling His promise to give the land to them (Joshua 4:19-24).

Next, Joshua had the Israelites circumcise themselves for the first time since the people left Egypt. By commanding this, God was confirming His covenant with Israel (Joshua 5:2-8). The site was named *Gilgal* (which sounds like the Hebrew for *roll*) because God said there, "Today I have rolled away the reproach of Egypt from you" (Joshua 5:9). The reproach was slavery, landlessness, the appearance that God had forsaken His promises. To celebrate God's faithfulness, Israel celebrated the first Passover in the promised land at Gilgal (Joshua 5:10-12).

Three centuries later, Gilgal was still a site of covenant ceremonies. There Israel confirmed Saul as the nation's first king (1 Samuel 11:14-15).

Thus, Gilgal signified that God had rolled away the shame of slavery and confirmed Israel as His chosen people under His covenant protection.

The day of the Lord (Amos 5:18). This is the earliest biblical reference to that day; the others are all in other prophetic books. We don't know exactly what Israel thought the day of the Lord was, but it probably meant the time when God would show Himself victorious over His opponents in the world. The Israelites apparently thought that they would be exalted when God's justice triumphed, as they were when God rolled away the shame of slavery in His victory over Egypt. Gilgal was a place of celebrating God's victories with assemblies like those described in Amos 5:21-23.

9. In contrast to Israel's expectations, 5:19 describes the day of the Lord in a vivid image. What does Amos mean in this verse?

10. What does it mean that the day of the Lord is "darkness" (5:18,20)?

Roll (5:24). In 5:21-24, the Lord explains again why He detests Israel's celebrations of the covenant. In doing so, He uses a peculiar Hebrew word. Nowhere else in the Old Testament is the word "roll" used of flowing water. The word sounds like "Gilgal."

Justice . . . righteousness (5:24). See the boxes on pages 34, 68, and 81.

Sacrifices (5:25). The Israelites did not grow crops or raise animals in the wilderness with Moses; they ate manna (Exodus 16). Therefore, they probably had nothing to sacrifice until they reached Gilgal.

For Further Study: **Compare Amos 5:25 to something that King Saul did at Gilgal, 1 Samuel 15:12-26. Note especially 15:22-23.**

For Thought and Discussion: **From 5:4-27, what heart attitudes show that a person has truly experienced God's transforming grace and is not just deceiving himself?**

Optional Application:
a. Meditate this week on Amos 5:24 and on God's standard of justice—Exodus 20:1-21 and/or Mark 12:29-31. Consider how you could apply this standard in your dealings with people.

b. Think about the meanings of justice and righteousness. Could you in any way let them "roll" more fully in your actions toward others this week? If you believe so, describe what you will make a point of doing. Consider what you owe your co-workers, family, neighbors, etc.

11. The Lord makes a pun between the sound of "Gilgal" and the sound of "roll" in 5:24. His point is that Gilgal means one kind of "rolling" to Israel but quite a different kind of "rolling" to Him. What kind of rolling should Israel do to really live up to the rolling the Lord did at Gilgal (5:24)?

12. To summarize chapter 5, name the three things the Lord wanted Israel to seek instead of religious experiences at holy places (5:6,14,24).

13. a. What insight from this chapter most strikes you as something you would like to apply to your own life?

b. How could you apply this insight? Describe any plans you have for prayer, meditation, or action.

14. List any questions you have about chapter 5.

For the group

Read aloud. When a passage is in distinct parts, as chapter 5 is, it can help to have a different person read each part. In this case, you might have someone read 5:1-3, another read 5:4-5, another 5:6-13, another 5:14-17, and another 5:18-27.

Summarize. Questions 1 and 12 both asked you to summarize the chapter. Hopefully, you were better able to do this at the end of your preparation than at the beginning. Use either question to draw the group to summarize chapter 5.

Before you look at the details of the chapter, make sure that everyone understands the framework of the three shrines. It may seem artificial because we have to have Amos' subtle allusions explained to us, whereas the Israelites would have caught his meaning immediately. A modern speaker might make allusions to television commercials or programs for the same reason. Also, this study guide oversimplifies the symbolism of each shrine to help Christians who are unfamiliar with them. In reality, the symbolism of Bethel or Gilgal to Israel was at least as complex as the symbolism of Hollywood to modern people.

Finally, be aware that not every commentator sees the symbolism of the three shrines in this chapter. You will have to decide for yourselves if this structure does or does not help you to understand what the Lord is saying in chapter 5.

Bethel. Look for all the signs of transformation in verses 6-13: turning justice into bitterness/wormwood (what does this mean?); changing the sky from summer to winter constellations; turning night into day; turning dry land into sea; and so on. Then look for Israel's failure to be transformed (5:11-13). What was the Lord's message for Israel, and what is His message for us?

Beersheba. The Lord alludes to "I will be with you" in 5:14 and 5:17. What is His point? If you grasped what He meant by "Seek me" in 5:6, how is that related to "Seek good" and "love good" in 5:14-15? How can you act on these commands?

Gilgal. The connection between 5:18-27 and Gilgal may be difficult to recognize in English. Gilgal symbolized victory, the same kind of victory that Israel expected on the day of the Lord. Likewise, Gilgal meant "roll"—God rolling away Israel's shame. But because Israel was not letting justice and righteousness "roll" (verse 24), the day of the Lord was going to be victory for the Lord but a return of Israel's shame.

If the Gilgal symbolism doesn't help you, let it go. Just try to see why the Israelites were longing for the day of the Lord and how their longing was wrong. Then look at what it means to let justice and righteousness roll. Finally, examine how you might put these lessons into practice.

Verses 25-26 are difficult. The Bible does not make plain whether Israel did begin to offer the sacrifices prescribed in the Law during the desert wandering, or whether the Israelites waited to offer sacrifices until they had flocks and crops to offer in the promised land. However, the Lord's point is probably clear enough: Israel's relationship with the Lord was not based primarily on sacrifices but on obedience and loyalty.

Summarize. Wrap up your discussion with a summary of the passage and a few key lessons you have learned that are applicable to your lives.

Worship. Seek the Lord in prayer, worshiping the God who transforms winter into summer, night into day, self-centered Jacobs into obedient Israels. Ask the Lord to be with you and to enable you to become what He desires you to be.

Justice and Righteousness, part three

If justice is the outward behavior of living by God's standard, then righteousness is the inner moral commitment to the relationship that motivates obedience to that standard. A man is righteous if he is living according to the outer and inner standards of the covenant relationship. This includes obedience to God's commands (justice) as well as living "without pride of heart, depending on Yahweh [the LORD] for protection and vindication."[4] Outward obedience alone will not put a person in the right relationship to God that the covenant describes. A person must also humbly trust God to provide all he needs, to forgive him when he inevitably fails to obey fully, and to enable him to grow more obedient. In short, the righteous man trusts in God's righteousness—God's commitment to His part of the covenant relationship. For God's part includes not merely justice, but also mercy, grace, and deliverance to the righteous man who seeks them.[5] (See Psalm 18:20-27, 37:1-17, 40:4-12; Matthew 5:20; Romans 3:21-26.)

1. Fee and Stuart, page 160.
2. Motyer, pages 105-137. See also J. M. Boice, "Amos," *The Minor Prophets: Volume 1: Hosea-Jonah* (Grand Rapids, Michigan: Zondervan Corporation, 1983), page 153-155.
3. Motyer, page 111.
4. D. Hill, *Greek Words and Hebrew Meanings: Studies in the Semantics of Soteriological Terms, Society for New Testament Studies Monograph Series 5,* pages 82-83.
5. Horst Seebass and Colin Brown, "Righteousness," *The New International Dictionary of New Testament Theology: Volume 3* (Grand Rapids, Michigan: Zondervan Corporation, 1978), pages 352-373.

LESSON SEVEN

AMOS 6:1-14

Complacency

In chapter 6, Amos culminates the Lord's legal indictment of Israel which he began in chapter 3. God has promised doom for those who turn "justice into bitterness" (5:7) yet hold religious celebrations and long for "the day of the LORD" (5:18). He has condemned those who claim the favor of the transforming God but are not transformed, who love evil but say that the One who hates evil is with them, who are sure that the covenant promises are theirs forever but have reduced the covenant acts to empty rituals. Now the Lord zeroes in on the sin behind all the rest, this time addressing the husbands of the "cows" (4:1) of Samaria.

As you read 6:1-14, look for the main point of this sermon.

Zion . . . Samaria (6:1). Amos addresses this woe to the leaders of both Judah and Israel.

Go to Calneh . . . (6:2). (See the map on page 9.) Hazael and Ben-Hadad of Damascus conquered large sections of Israel, but Jeroboam II recovered all of Israel's lost territory and even took effective control over Damascus itself. Jeroboam's army may well have taken Calneh and Hamath (2 Kings 14:23-29); King Uzziah of Judah had taken Gath (2 Chronicles 26:6). In Amos 6:2-3, the Lord seems to be mimicking the way "the people of Israel" were flattering their "notable men" (6:1). Or, the Lord is mimicking the secret thoughts with which the notable men were flattering themselves.

Lo Debar (6:13). A city regained for Israel by King Jehoash (2 Kings 10:32-33, 13:25). The actual Hebrew phrase Amos uses is *lo dabar,* which means "nothing". He may be punning on the name of this city, of which Israel was so proud.

Karnaim (6:13). Another city retaken by Jehoash. *Karnaim* means "horns"—symbols of strength.

---

1. Read the Lord's mimicking in 6:1-2,13. How were the leaders of Israel and Judah flattering themselves or being flattered?

2. What do you learn about these men's characters (values, priorities) from 6:4-6?

3. Verses 1 and 8 sum up the men's attitudes as complacency (RSV: ease) and pride (NASB: arrogance; KJV: excellency). What do these words mean? (Use a dictionary if necessary.)

   complacency

pride ____

____

____

____

Reign of terror (6:3). Literally, "seat of violence." This prediction indeed came to pass. Between Jeroboam's death in 753 and Israel's destruction in 723, the nation had six rulers, most of whom died violently. Israel's political might and commercial prosperity both collapsed; Assyria conquered all the cities named in Amos 6. (See the box, "Israel after Amos" on pages 88-90.)

Joseph (6:6). The northern kingdom of Israel was dominated by the tribe of Ephraim, who was Joseph's son. Therefore, Israel was sometimes called Joseph.

Do horses . . . oxen (6:12). Since horseshoes were unknown in Amos' day, everyone knew it would be foolish to take a horse on the sharp cliffs of Israel. Likewise, it would have been absurd to have oxen plow there (or on the sea, as in RSV).[1]

---

4. Although Israel knew how to use horses and oxen, what foolish things was the nation doing (6:12-13)?

____

____

____

____

____

____

5. Why was Israel foolish to "feel secure" (6:1) because of its "fortresses" (6:8), its size and affluence (6:2), and its military successes (6:13)? Consider 6:8,11,14.

For Thought and Discussion: a. When leaders are complacent, arrogant, preoccupied by pleasure and comfort, and indifferent to the acts and needs of their people (6:1-2,4-6), then they make anarchy eventually inevitable (6:3). Why does this kind of leadership make ruin inevitable?

b. Do you see any similar leaders bringing similar ruin on their people in your own day? If so, how might you pray for those leaders and those people?

Lebo Hamath . . . Arabah (6:14). From Israel's northern border to its southern border (2 Kings 14:25).

6. What attitudes does it seem that the Lord wanted Israel's leaders to have about . . .

   the nation's prosperity, and their own?

   their responsibilities as leaders?

7. How would you summarize Amos' message in 6:1-14?

Your response

8. Are you tempted to feel secure in anything besides a close relationship with God? If you suspect so, explain what that temptation is. (Think for a few moments about what you strongly feel you need.)

9. The goals of Israel's leaders were possessions, power, comfort, and praise from people. Do you need to take any steps currently to keep your goals in line with God's desires? If so, describe those steps.

10. List any questions you have about chapter 6.

For the group

This chapter is chiefly about the sins of pride and complacency, feeling secure in ultimately insecure things. A possible structure for your discussion is:

For Further Study: Review 3:1-6:14, and summarize the Lord's reasons for declaring war on Israel.

What is pride? What is complacency?
How did the leaders of Israel show pride and complacency?
Why are pride and complacency foolish, and why do they anger the Lord?
What results did the Lord promise for these attitudes?
What are you tempted to feel proud or complacent about?
How can Christians avoid pride and complacency?

It might be helpful to wrap up your discussion with a summary of the Lord's charges against Israel in chapters 3-6. If He seemed cruel and judgmental on your first reading, does He now seem justified in ending His patience with Israel. Have you learned anything about the need for Christ?

Israel after Amos

During the years when Amos prophesied, sometime between 760 and 753 BC, Israel was at its highest prosperity and security since Solomon died. But after Jeroboam II died in 753 BC, everything fell apart.

Jeroboam's son Zechariah succeeded his father and proceeded to behave like a pagan prince. Careless luxury, cruelty, empty religion, and pride continued. But Zechariah, no talented ruler like his father, never gained control over Israel's greedy, unscrupulous aristocrats. One of them named Shallum murdered Zechariah after six months.

With the legal heir dead, the other aristocrats regarded the throne as up for grabs. Shallum held on for only a month until an aristocrat named Menahem led his private army to Samaria, quickly killed Shallum, and took control of Samaria. Determined to hold his throne, Menahem was ruthless against those who resisted his claim to kingship. He sacked one city that refused him, and even had pregnant women ripped open in the manner of a pagan conqueror (2 Kings 15:16). Menahem's determination succeeded, and he reigned from 752 until he died

(continued on page 89)

(continued from page 88)
naturally in 742.

About this time, Assyria's new ruler, Tiglath-Pileser, was whipping his army into the most effective fighting force yet seen in the world. Jeroboam had been lucky that Assyria was sleeping; his successors were not so lucky. Tiglath-Pileser marched his army to Israel's border, but Menahem bought him off with about 37 tons of silver by taxing about 60,000 wealthy Israelites (2 Kings 15:20).[2] Assyria's purchased support secured Menahem's throne until his death.

When Menahem's son Pekahiah succeeded him in 742 BC, the same religious and social sins Amos had warned against twenty years earlier were still going on. The prophet Hosea had taken on the task of warning Israel, but no one was listening. After two years, one of Pekahiah's officers, Pekah, took over the palace in a military coup.

Pekah kept a grip on Israel from 740 to 732, but his foreign policy was disastrous. He favored the anti-Assyrian faction at court, and so he allied with Rezin of Damascus to oust Assyria. Pekah and Rezin even attacked King Ahaz of Judah to force him to join their rebellion, but Ahaz appealed to Tiglath-Pileser for help (2 Kings 16:5-14, Isaiah 7:1-11:16).

The Assyrian king was happy to oblige. He swept south, conquering Damascus and all of Israel except a small area around Samaria between 738 and 732. At that point, a pro-Assyrian named Hoshea murdered Pekah and immediately paid Tiglath-Pileser tribute to spare Samaria.

Tiglath-Pileser was brutal to his conquered territories. "Corpses impaled on stakes, severed heads stacked in heaps, and captives skinned alive"[3] provided psychological terror. Tiglath-Pileser deported thousands of Israel's more educated and wealthy citizens to other parts of the Near East and replaced them with non-Israelites from elsewhere. The Assyrian goal was to prevent nationalistic uprisings; the Lord's goal was to fulfill His promises.

(continued on page 90)

(continued from page 89)

When Tiglath-Pileser died in 727, Hoshea decided he no longer had to pay tribute. However, Assyria's new king felt differently. After a cruel three-year siege from 725 to 723, Samaria fell to starvation and battering rams. King Sargon of Assyria recorded deporting 27,290 captives, leaving some farmers to produce taxable crops. Israel as a nation was demolished; ten of the original twelve tribes no longer existed; Amos' prophecy from 1:1-9:10 was fulfilled after just thirty years.[4]

1. Martin-Achard, page 50; Mays, pages 120-121.
2. *The NIV Study Bible*, page 552.
3. *The NIV Study Bible*, page 550.
4. This history summarizes 2 Kings 15:8-17:41. See also *The NIV Study Bible*, pages 548-558; Madelein S. and J. Lane Miller, *Harper's Encyclopedia of Bible Life* (San Francisco: Harper and Row, 1978), pages 314-315.

LESSON EIGHT

AMOS 7:1-17

The Plumb Line Test

First the Lion roared His warning: Wrath was approaching the chosen people, who were no better than the pagans despite the Lord's revelations to them (1:1-2:16). Next He declared war on His rebel subjects, bringing formal charges against them but still promising to recall His army if the nation would repent (3:1-6:14). But with the end of chapter 6, the time of patience ended: The Lion was pouncing, the trap was snapping shut, the attackers were on the march (3:4-6). Was the Lord canceling His covenant? He gave Amos the five visions of chapters 7 through 9 to answer this question.

As you read 7:1-17, consider how it helps to shape the theme of Amos' message.

Vision (7:1-9)

Locusts . . . fire (7:1,4). Locusts were the most disastrous plague known in the Near East, and they were traditionally considered punishment from God. The divine fire was a symbol of the Lord's wrath.[1]

The king's share (7:1). Apparently, the first grass crop of each year went to the state as a tax.[2]

1. The Lord first showed Amos "swarms of locusts" devouring the plants upon which Israel's life

depended (7:1-2). In your own words, explain what Amos did in response to the vision, and how the Lord responded to Amos.

2. The second vision reinforces the first, stressing the common message.

Describe the attitudes toward the Lord and Israel behind each part of Amos' prayers. You could contrast these attitudes with those the people had been showing.

"Sovereign LORD" (verses 2,5)

"forgive!" (verse 2)

"stop!" (verse 5)

"He is so small." (verses 2,5)

3. Read the box, "Prophetic Intercession," on page 99.

   a. Amos 7:3,6 says that "the LORD relented" in response to Amos' prayer. How can prayer be effective and necessary when God is sovereign over all that happens and changeless in His nature?

   b. The Old Testament prophets were singled out to receive the Holy Spirit partly in order that they might pray for God's will to be done. How do Christians have any similar responsibility? (*Optional*: See Matthew 6:9-10, Romans 8:26-27, Ephesians 6:11-12,18-20.)

Optional Application: Ask God to show you whether you should commit yourself to a ministry of intercession, and if so, how you should go about it. What is His will, and how could your prayer help Him to bring it about?

For Thought and Discussion: a. Could any Israelite have passed the plumb line test? Consider Genesis 15:6, and Psalms 32, 130 and 131.

b. How does Jesus' death solve the problem that the plumb line test presents to mankind (Romans 3:21-26, 5:6-11, 7:21-8:4)?

For Further Study: Compare Amos' vision of the plumb line to Paul's description of how we should build the Church (1 Corinthians 3:9-17). How is the foundation of the Church (3:11) like the foundation on which Israel was built? How do Paul's instructions for building resemble the plumb line test (3:12-15)?

Plumb line (7:7). A lead weight on a cord, used for measuring whether a building is perfectly vertical. The leaning tower of Pisa is perfectly straight, but it is not vertical, not "true to plumb."

4. What building was the Lord planning to measure with His plumb line (7:8-9)?

5. What does the plumb line symbolize? That is, by what standard was the Lord going to measure whether the nation was built upright? (*Optional*: See Leviticus 19:18; Deuteronomy 5:6-26; 6:4-6; Isaiah 28:16-17; Amos 5:4,14-15,24.)

6. Amos did not ask the Lord not to use His plumb line. How did the judgment by plumb line differ from the judgments by locusts and fire which the Lord rejected?

7. How would you summarize the point of 7:1-9?

Vision vindicated (7:10-17)

Bethel was the main center of worship in the kingdom of Israel, since the people were not allowed to go to worship in Jerusalem. Israel's kings supported the cult at Bethel, and in exchange the Bethel priests preached that the Lord loved Israel and its king. This was religion in the service of politics at its purest.

Amaziah was apparently the chief priest of Bethel. Amos was delivering his prophesies perhaps at the very door of Amaziah's temple, where everyone who came to worship could hear. This was more than Amaziah could stand.

8. Did Amaziah owe his chief loyalty to the Lord or to someone else? How can you tell (7:10,13)?

9. How did Amaziah try to move Amos to abandon his mission (7:10-13)? To what desires and feelings did he appeal?

Optional Application: Measure your own life according to God's plumb line for Christians. You might meditate on Exodus 20:1-17 and/or John 15:12-13. What confession or other action does this measurement lead you to?

For Further Study: Compare Amaziah's reaction to Amos with the Pharisees' reaction to Jesus (Luke 11:37-54).

For Thought and Discussion: Why is it easy for religious leaders to take Amaziah's attitude toward their critics? What can the Church do to make this kind of confrontation less divisive?

For Thought and Discussion: Think about Mark 12:29-31. Did Amos measure up to the Lord's plumb line test? Why or why not?

A prophet's son (7:14). While most people in Israel and Judah were indifferent to the Lord, communities of people gathered together "for the purpose of mutual edification and the cultivation of the experience of God."[3] These men were called "the sons of the prophets" (1 Kings 20:35; 2 Kings 2:3,5,7,15; 4:1,38; 5:22; 6:1; 9:1). A community of disciples often gathered around a mature prophet, who acted as their mentor. Elisha, for example, was Elijah's closest disciple for many years before he succeeded Elijah as Israel's chief prophet.

By contrast, Amos says he was neither another prophet's disciple, nor did he set out to become a prophet on his own.

10. How was Amos authorized to preach against the legitimate government and the official religion of Israel (7:14-15)?

____

____

____

____

11. Amos' life was in danger because Amaziah had told the king that he was fomenting treason (7:10). Nevertheless, Amos rejected the priest's order to leave the country and repeated the Lord's message to Amaziah's face (7:16-17). What does Amos' response to Amaziah tell you about his priorities, concerns, and goals?

____

____

____

____

____

____

Your response

12. What do you learn from 7:1-17 about what a committed Christian should be and do?

13. How could you act on something you have seen in chapter 7 that applies to you?

14. List any questions you have about 7:1-17.

For the group

Summarize. At this point, you may want to summarize 7:1-9 and 7:10-17 separately. The connection between the two passages may be more clear after you have discussed them. Look for the answer to this question in chapters 7-9: "Is the Lord abandoning His covenant with Israel?"

For Thought and Discussion: Paul told Timothy, "everyone who wants to live a godly life in Christ Jesus will be persecuted" (2 Timothy 3:12). Paul had in mind not just teasing and nagging but slander, economic discrimination, social rejection, lawsuits, physical attack, and even imprisonment, torture, and death. Why must truly godly living (active obedience to God) lead to persecution?

Optional Application: How could you imitate Amos' commitment to his mission from God despite rejection and danger?

For Further Study: Add chapter 7 to your outline of Amos. Let your subtitles show how each section relates to the overall message of the book.

Locust and fire. The main issues here are the character the Lord reveals in 7:1-6, the attitudes Amos shows in his prayers, and the purpose of intercessory prayer. To see the Lord's character, note the kinds of judgment He abandons and the apparent reasons why He reveals His intentions to Amos. Question 2 deals with the attitudes of prayer, and question 3 with the purpose of intercession. For application, ask whether the Lord reveals His intentions to Christians so that they might pray. Are His character and methods the same as they were in Amos' day?

Plumb line. The plumb line test is God's standard of justice and righteousness, the terms of the covenant, expressed above all in passages like the Ten Commandments. Make sure that this symbolism is clear to everyone from the passage. Then consider how this method of judgment is different from the judgment by locust or fire. How does this method help you better understand the Lord's character? What kind of a Judge is He?

The plumb line test is applicable to Christians in some ways and not others. For one thing, Christ died because all of us have failed the test. For us, passing the test of righteousness means relying on Christ's righteousness rather than our own. Also, the Holy Spirit was given to us so that we might learn to pass the test with His power. These are difficult truths to summarize in a few sentences, but well worth discussing.

Amos and Amaziah. Amos inserted this passage here apparently because it deals with the religious authorities' response to the prophecy in verse 9. The main lessons for us are the characters displayed by the religious leader and the prophet. Look at the one as an example of attitudes to avoid, and the other as an example of attitudes to adopt.

Summarize. By now you should have a fair understanding of what an Old Testament prophet was. How is it like and unlike your previous notion of what a prophet was? To what extent is the prophet's role applicable to the Church today?

Worship. Thank the Lord for responding to the prayers of believers. Thank Him that in His eternal changelessness and sovereignty over the world, He accomplishes His aims through the prayers of believers who can choose to pray. Ask Him to show you how you might serve His purposes through your prayers.

Prophetic Intercession

The Lord revealed His plans to a prophet partly so that he might report the Lord's plans to the people. But the job of "king's herald" was only part of the prophet's office. The Lord sometimes revealed His intentions so that the prophet might intercede for the people in prayer. The Bible often calls this prophetic function "standing in the breach." See Genesis 18:16-33, 20:7; 1 Kings 13:4-6, 17:19-24; 2 Kings 4:32-35; Psalm 106:21-23; Isaiah 37:1-4; Jeremiah 7:16; Ezekiel 13:4-5, 22:30-31.

The prophets were not the only Old Testament people who interceded for others. However, since the Holy Spirit had not yet been poured out to all God's people, the prophets were intimate with the Lord in a way that few other people were.[4]

1. Mays, pages 28, 131.
2. Motyer, page 153; *The NIV Study Bible*, page 1356.
3. *The NIV Study Bible*, page 517.
4. Mays, page 130; "Amos," *Matthew Henry's Commentary on the Whole Bible* (New York: Revell, n.d.).

LESSON NINE

AMOS 8:1-14

The Time is Ripe

In his third vision (7:7-9), Amos learned that the Lord was going to measure Israel by the "plumb line" of justice and righteousness—by the outer and inner standards of the covenant relationship. Knowing that the people would not measure up, the Lord revealed the destruction that persistent disobedience had made inevitable.

Amos' fourth vision is of "a basket of ripe fruit" (8:1). In Hebrew, the words *fruit* and *end* sound the same; the Lord uses the sight of the one to suggest the other. NASB and KJV translate verse 2 literally: "summer fruit . . . the end has come. . . ." NIV tries to show the sense of the pun by translating: "ripe fruit . . . the time is ripe. . . ."

As you read 8:1-14, try to relate it to the rest of Amos' message.

1. What did the Lord say to Amos through the basket of fruit (8:2)?

____

____

____

____

____

2. The Lord's plumb line test had to do with justice toward God and neighbor, as defined in the

Ten Commandments. Israel owed certain attitudes and behavior toward God, and certain ones toward other people. The test also had to do with righteous humility about one's own weaknesses and the Lord's strength and graciousness.

How had Israel failed the plumb line test (8:4-6)?

____

____

____

____

____

3. The time of ripe fruit at summer's end was harvest time. This was normally a time of festival revelry for Israel, but the Lord promised that His harvest of judgment would bring a different mood (8:3,9-10). What did He promise?

____

____

____

____

____

Pride of Jacob (8:7). The Lord Himself was sometimes called the Pride of Jacob, since the Hebrew word also means "majesty." Israel took pride in having the Lord as its God, but it was a false, self-satisfied pride that assumed the blessing was deserved.

Rise like the Nile (8:8). Heavy seasonal rains in Ethiopia, at the Nile's source, flooded the river yearly. The river rose by as much as 25 feet, flooding the whole valley except the villages built above it. It stirred up rich soil from the river bottom and deposited it on the land when the river subsided.[1]

4. a. Verse 8 reveals one consequence of sin. Describe this result of man's self-centeredness. (*Optional*: See Genesis 3:17-18, Isaiah 24:5, Jeremiah 3:1-3, Romans 8:20.)

____

____

____

____

____

b. Verse 8 also describes the effects of Israel's attitudes (8:4-6) on the human community. How does a society "rise like the Nile" and become "stirred up and then sink like the river of Egypt" when people reject God's standards of justice and righteousness?

____

____

____

____

____

Sackcloth . . . shave your heads (8:10). Signs of mourning.

Sea to sea and . . . north to east (8:12). From the Dead Sea to the Mediterranean and all over Israel; everywhere but south to Jerusalem where the Lord's Temple was, where prophets still spoke, and where Scripture was still read.

Shame (8:14). "Guilt" in NASB; "sin" in KJV. The Hebrew word is *ashimah*, the same as the name of a Syrian goddess (RSV reads "Ashimah"). The god of Dan and the god of Beersheba were supposedly the Lord, but the people's notions of Him were so mixed with ideas of pagan gods that they were not really worshiping the Lord at all.

For Thought and Discussion: The people would not find the word of the Lord, even though they would seek almost everywhere for it (8:12). Why were the seekers not going to find it (Isaiah 59:4,9-10; Romans 1:18, 21-22)?

For Thought and Discussion: The young people brought up by Amos' audience were going to faint for thirst (8:13) for lack of God's truth. How does one generation's rebellion affect the next generation?

5. a. The Lord reveals another result of rejecting the plumb line of the Word of God (8:11-14). What is that result?

____

____

____

____

b. The current generation did not want to hear God's words through Amos (7:16), but changed circumstances would make people hunger for God's words. In what way do circumstances sometimes affect people's interest in listening to God?

____

____

____

____

____

c. How were people going to try to quench their thirst for spiritual truth when circumstances made them thirsty (8:14)?

____

____

____

____

6. Summarize the message of 8:1-14.

____

____

____

____

____

7. Do you think the world today resembles Amos' prediction in 8:1-14 in any ways? If so, describe all the similarities you see.

Optional Application: Intercede with the Lord on behalf of your own nation. Ask Him to reveal in you any attitudes like the ones Amos condemns.

8. a. Second Chronicles 7:14 explains the first actions a Christian should take when faced with a problem in his or her society. What actions does that verse recommend?

b. When approaching a problem of your society, why should you begin with the attitudes of Nehemiah 1:7, Psalm 51:10, and Psalm 139:23-24?

9. Does Amos' warning in 8:1-14 prompt you to any prayer or other action? If so, what in his words seems applicable to you, and what do you plan to do about it?

For Further Study: Add titles for chapter 8's subsections to your outline of Amos.

____

____

____

____

10. Write down any questions you have about chapter 8.

____

____

____

____

For the group

In this chapter, the Lord takes a last look at the sins that made Israel ripe for judgment (8:4-6), and He names a few of the consequences that Israel's sin is going to bring (8:3, 8:8, 8:9-10, 8:11-14). Although the Lord says that He will send the consequences, at the same time they are the natural, just results of Israel's choices.

Take a look at Israel's sin, and ask yourselves whether you see similar attitudes among Christians or nonChristians today. Then consider each of the consequences in turn. Why is it a fair result of sin? Do you see signs of similar results today? What can Christians do to stem the tide of disaster that persistent sin invites?

You might end your meeting by praying for your community, nation, and/or world. Ask the Lord to show you how to pray and act to divert or temper judgment.

Old Testament Prophets, part three

Israel had prophets from Moses onward, but few of their writings appear in the Old Testament. We know nothing of the prophets during the period of the judges, from Joshua to Samuel, about

(continued on page 107)

(continued from page 106)
1400 to 1058 BC.[2] From the books of Samuel and Kings we know a bit about the words and lives of prophets like Samuel, Nathan, Micaiah, Elijah, and Elisha, who lived between 1058 and 800 BC. These men spoke God's current word about obedience to the covenant in their times. They may well have delivered prophecies like those in Amos' book, but their prophecies were not written down.

The prophets whose books appear in the Old Testament, from Isaiah to Malachi, lived between 800 and 400 BC. Amos was one of the earliest. Why did God want the oracles of only these prophets written down in the Bible? We cannot know His full reasons, but we can see some purposes. These were times of "1) unprecedented political, military, economic, and social upheaval, 2) an enormous level of religious unfaithfulness and disregard for the original Mosaic covenant, and 3) shifts in populations and national boundaries."[3]

Israel's extreme sin made extreme judgment necessary under the terms of the covenant. The Lord destroyed Israel, then demolished Judah, then miraculously restored Judah from exile, then abandoned Judah to conquerors for centuries, and finally sent His own Son to pay the covenant price for the people's sin. The prophets' writings record for us why the covenant demanded these acts of justice. The writings also show that the Lord had planned His acts of mercy all along.

1. *The NIV Study Bible*, page 1357.
2. J. I. Packer, Merrill C. Tenney, and William White, Jr., *The World of the Old Testament* (Nashville: Thomas Nelson, 1982), pages 43-48. Other scholars date Joshua's entry into the promised land around 1200 BC.
3. Fee and Stuart, page 157.

LESSON TEN

AMOS 9:1-15

Destruction . . . and Beyond

The sieve (9:1-10)

In his fifth vision, Amos beholds the climax of the Lord's wrath, either at Jerusalem[1] or Bethel.[2] In either case, the altar was supposed to be the place where the Lord accepted a sacrifice to substitute for the guilty people, the place where He could therefore have mercy on His people, the place where peace with God and blessing from God were restored. The Lord's presence above the altar was supposed to signify His favor and intimacy. But now the Lord was promising to level the temple, to destroy the place of mercy. Beginning with the temple, judgment would spread throughout the land.

Read 9:1-10.

1. According to 9:1-4, who would escape the Lord's wrath?

____

____

2. a. How was Israel special to the Lord (2:9-11, 3:1-2)?

____

____

____

____

For Thought and Discussion: a. In what ways was Israel the same to the Lord as the Cushites/Ethiopians (9:7)? (Amos 1:3-2:16 shows one way.)

b. In what ways is a Christian special to the Lord? What should be a Christian's attitude toward his specialness? How should he treat God and other people in light of his specialness?

b. By delivering Israel from Egypt, the Lord proved His special love for Israel. The covenant relationship was based on that unearned act of grace. However, Israel had acquired a wrong attitude about its special relationship, and now the Lord had to remind Israel that He had given new land and freedom to pagan peoples also (9:7).

What wrong attitude about being special to God was He condemning in 9:7?

____

____

____

____

____

3. What two promises did the Lord make in 9:8?

a. ______________________________

____

____

b. ______________________________

____

____

Kernel (9:9). KJV reads "grain"; NASB reads "kernel" or "pebble"; NIV © 1984 reads "pebble"; RSV reads "pebble." "In threshing, wheat was first beaten or shredded on the threshing floor to separate the grains from the stalk and husk, then winnowed to allow the light chaff to blow to one side. The remaining grain would contain trash and small stones. The large mesh sieve was used to catch the larger debris and let the smaller grains fall through. The primary point is catching the undesirable."[3]

The trash, the pebbles, the sinners, will be caught in the Lord's sieve and destroyed, but the grain will be saved. (Compare Matthew

13:24-30.) If KJV is correct that no *grain* will fall through, then Amos means that no one will be saved or that no good grain will be lost.[4]

---

4. In 9:1-4, the Lord stresses that "not one" of the people will escape His wrath. In 9:8 He says that He will "not totally destroy the house of Jacob." He resolves this apparent paradox in 9:9-10 with the metaphor of the sieve.

   a. How is the sieve like the plumb line?

   b. How does the sieve show why 9:8 does not contradict 9:1-4?

5. Summarize the message of 9:1-10.

For Thought and Discussion: The sinners who are caught in the sieve are those who say, "Disaster will not overtake or meet us" (9:10). Explain this sinful attitude in your own words.

Restoration (9:11-15)

Study Skill—Prophetic Forms, part three

Amos 9:11-15 follows a form called the *promise* or *salvation* oracle. The form includes reference to the future ("In that day . . . ," verse 11), radical change (repair of David's tent, exaltation over Edom, return from exile, verses 11-15), and blessing. The blessings are the ones promised in the covenant (Deuteronomy 28:1-14)—life, health, prosperity, agricultural abundance, respect, and safety.[5] Other salvation oracles are Hosea 2:16-23, Isaiah 45:1-7, and Jeremiah 31:1-9.

Even the Jews knew that Amos 9:11-15 was about the kingdom that the Messiah, the Christ, would bring when He came to reign. However, the passage does not answer all our questions about heaven, the millenium, and so on. Therefore, we need to study 9:11-15 for what it does tell us, and look for answers to our other questions in other passages. When the Lord chooses not to satisfy our curiosity about the end times, we need to be content to wait.

Also, in promise oracles the Lord frequently uses symbolism to make His point. "David's fallen tent," "the remnant of Edom," and the new wine dripping from the mountains all represent certain things, for example. Therefore, when we try to unravel 9:11-15, we should use the Holy Spirit's guidance, other passages of Scripture, and common sense to determine when the Lord is speaking literally and when symbolically, and what the symbols mean. Even if we cannot be certain about our understanding of the details, the overall point of the prophecy is clear enough to motivate us to act in faith today.

As you read 9:11-15, notice how these verses expand upon the note of hope in 9:8, the glory that will arise from the destruction on the day of the Lord. Ask God to guide your understanding.

Tent (9:11). "Tabernacle" in KJV; "booth" in RSV and NASB. Originally, this was the kind of tent in which nomads lived as they herded their flocks from pasture to pasture. The Israelites lived in such tents in the desert for forty years after the Exodus, but they largely turned to houses after they entered the promised land. One special tent was built to house the Lord's presence during the wilderness wandering; this tent was often called "the tabernacle of the LORD" or "the tent of meeting." After the Israelites entered the promised land and began to build houses, they were commanded to commemorate their desert wandering by living in the traditional tents for one week each year. This commemoration was called "the Feast of Booths" or "the Feast of Tabernacles."

"David's fallen tent" (9:11) is David's fallen house. Calling it a tent stresses its flimsiness.

For Thought and Discussion: Amos saw the far future as though it were all simultaneous, but from our perspective we know that some of his prophecy has been fulfilled, and some has not. Verses 1:1-9:10 have been fulfilled. Has any part of 9:11-15 been fulfilled? What light does the New Testament shed on your understanding of 9:11-15?

6. What is the Lord promising in 9:11?

____

____

____

____

7. The Lord says that Israel will "possess the remnant of Edom" (9:12), those who remain after Edom is destroyed (1:11-12). Whom does "the remnant of Edom" represent, and what does it mean that Israel will "possess" them? (*Optional*: See Isaiah 56:6-8, 60:10-14.)

____

____

____

____

____

For Further Study: Compare the results of covenant relationship described in 9:11-15 to the results of rebellion described in 5:11 and 8:8.

For Thought and Discussion: The Lord calls Himself "your God" only in 4:12 and 9:15. What do you learn from the fact that He ends Amos' prophecy by calling Himself "your God"?

8. To bear someone's name or be called by someone's name means to belong to someone. Who are "the nations [or, Gentiles] that bear my name" (9:12)?

9. What results of the restoration of the covenant relationship does the Lord promise in 9:13-15?

10. The curse upon the land and Israel's eventual expulsion from the land were the nation's just rewards for sin. What do the words "never again" in 9:15 imply about the people after the restoration of the kingdom?

Your response

11. What do you learn about the Lord from 9:1-15?

12. What is the most important insight you have had from your study of 9:1-15?

13. Does anything in this chapter prompt you to some prayer or action? If so, how are you prompted to respond?

14. List any questions you have about chapter 9.

Optional Application: What privileges, hopes, and responsibilities are yours because the Sovereign Lord is "your God"?

For the group

The sieve. The main issue in 9:1-10 is Israel's election. Was the Lord planning to cast everyone in Israel out of His covenant people, or would a faithful few be saved? What attitudes should a person chosen by God have toward God and others? What does the Lord's use of the plumb line or sieve tell you about Him?

Restoration. The box on page 117 is included to help Christians respond to a common criticism of biblical prophecy. Potential Christians and young Christians often need us to explain why we believe what we believe (1 Peter 3:15). However, disregard the box if it raises an issue that is unimportant to you because you know that Scripture is God's trustworthy Word.

Before you try to analyze each phrase in 9:11-15 for what it can tell you about the future, step back and look at the purpose of the passage. What can you say for certain about what it means? How should it motivate you to think and act in the present? What can it tell you about the Lord?

When you have grasped the point of the passage as a whole, then look at the individual statements. Here are some of the phrases you might examine:

restore David's fallen tent
possess the remnant of Edom and the nations that bear my name
the reaper will be overtaken by the plowman
new wine will drip from the mountains
I will bring back . . . Israel
they will rebuild/live in . . . plant/drink . . . make/eat
I will plant . . . never again to be uprooted
the Lord your God

It will take some discernment not to take symbolically what the Lord means literally, and not to take literally what the Lord means symbolically.

Worship. Thank God for the hope He has promised those who trust Him. Thank Him for each thing He has promised. Ask Him to enable you to act today in light of the glory that awaits you.

The Integrity of the Prophetic Books

Many commentators think that Amos could not have written 9:11-15 because "a prophecy is earlier than what it predicts, but contemporary with, or later than what it presupposes."[6] The kingdom of Judah did not fall until 586 BC, but Amos speaks as though it has already fallen and he is seeing beyond its fall. Therefore, someone must have added 9:11-15 after 586 BC. However, there are two answers to this theory. First, Amos may mean that David's tent fell when the tribes of Israel split from the tribes of Judah. Second, since Amos prophesies the fall of Jerusalem in 2:4-5, he could certainly presuppose that fall and look beyond it. The Lord had to reveal the fall before He revealed the restoration, but Amos' book shows that the Lord revealed both to Amos.

1. *The NIV Study Bible*, page 1358.
2. Mays, page 152; Motyer, 193-194; Martin-Achard, page 62.
3. Mays, page 161.
4. *Matthew Henry's Commentary*.
5. Fee and Stuart, pages 160-161.
6. G. E. Wright, *Isaiah* (Atlanta: John Knox Press, 1964), page 8.

LESSON ELEVEN

REVIEW

For Further Study: Complete an outline of the book of Amos, as detailed as you like.

Now that you've studied Amos in detail, do you have a firm grasp of the book as a whole? If your head is full of a jumble of details, a review can help you sort out what you've learned.

1. First, reread the whole book if possible. It should be familiar to you by now, so you should be able to skim, looking for threads that tie the book together. Pray for a fresh perspective on what God is saying. This may sound like a lot of work, but it will help you to remember. Don't get bogged down; just do what you can.

2. Look back at the outline on page 18, any outlines you have made of individual passages, and the summaries you wrote at the end of each lesson in this study guide. With these to help you, summarize the message of each of the book's three main sections.

   1:2-2:16 ______________________________

   ____

   ____

   ____

   ____

   3:1-6:14 ______________________________

   ____

7:1-9:15

3. In lesson one, you stated what seemed to be the main message of the book. After studying the book in detail, have you changed your mind? Remembering the main ideas of the three sections, what do you now think God was saying to Israel through Amos?

4. What did you learn from the book of Amos about . . .

   who God is?

   election (being chosen by God)?

what God expects of His people?

judgment?

justice and righteousness?

the prophet's role in Israel?

the need for Christ? ____________________

____

____

____

____

____

5. Did you learn anything else that seems important to remember? If so, what?

____

____

____

____

____

____

____

6. What have you learned about yourself from your study of Amos?

____

____

____

____

____

7. Have you noticed any areas (thoughts, attitudes, opinions, behavior) in which you have changed as a result of studying Amos? If so, how have you changed?

____

____

____

8. Look back over the entire study at questions in which you expressed a desire to make some application. Are you satisfied with your follow-through? Pray about any of those areas that you think you should continue to pursue specifically. (Now that you have completed this study, perhaps something new has come to mind that you would like to concentrate on. If so, bring it before God in prayer as well.) Write any notes here.

9. Review the questions you listed at the ends of lessons one through ten. Do any questions that seem important to you remain unanswered? If so, some of the sources on pages 127-131 may help answer some of your questions. Or, you might study some particular passage with cross-references on your own.

For the group

Read aloud. If you feel it would take too long to read the whole book of Amos aloud, try choosing four or five passages to be read aloud. These will remind everyone of the flavor of Amos' book. Some possibilities are 1:2-5; 2:6-8; 3:1-2; 4:11-13; 5:4-6,14-15,24; 6:1,14; 7:7-9; 8:1-2; 9:1,8,11-15.

Main message. Questions 2 and 3 ask you to summarize first the three main sections and then the whole book. Try to come up with the clearest statements you can. Anyone who has an outline in his study Bible or commentary might offer it as one person's view.

Themes. This should be the heart of your discussion. You can combine questions 4 through 7 as follows:

Consider the first theme, what you learned about God. Take about five minutes to list everything you learned, then turn to application. Let group members share how what they learned about God has affected their attitudes and actions. Ask if anyone has plans to pursue further action in response to what you have learned about God.

Then treat the next theme—election—in the same way, and so on through the list. Skip any items you all agree to skip in the interest of time.

Questions. Be sure to allow time for group members to raise questions that remain unanswered (question 9). As a general rule, the group leader should never do what the group can do for itself, so it would be better to direct people to sources where they can find answers than just to answer their questions. Better still, let the group answer an individual's questions.

Evaluation. Take a few minutes or a whole meeting to evaluate how your group functioned during your study of Amos. Some questions you might ask are:

How well did the study help you to grasp the book of Amos?
What were the most important truths you discovered together about the Lord?
What did you like best about your meetings?
What did you like least? What would you change?
How well did you meet the goals you set at your first meeting?
What did you learn about small group study?
What are members' current needs and interests?
What will you do next?

Worship. Thank God for specific things He has taught you about Himself and you, and for specific ways He has matured you through your study of Amos. Thank Him for the opportunity to meet and study the Bible together. Ask Him to guide you as to what to do next as a group.

GOING ON IN AMOS

Ideas for Further Study

1. Study the idea of *justice* in . . .

   a. the Law. First see Deuteronomy 5:1-21, 6:4-9. Then look at applications of the Ten Commandments to Israelite life in Deuteronomy 12-26, especially 15:1-18, 16:18-20, 17:8-20, 19:1-21, 21:1-23, 22:1-30, 24:1-22, and 25:1-16.

   b. the Prophets. See Isaiah 5:8-30, 10:1-4, 11:1-9, 28:1-29, 42:1-9, and 59:1-21. Then look up other references to justice in a concordance.

   c. the New Testament. Romans 13:1-10 is a key passage. Most of the New Testament assumes the Old Testament standard of justice and teaches us to go beyond it to self-sacrificing love. See Luke 6:27-38.

2. Study the names of God Amos uses. Consider why he chooses the one he does in each instance.

3. Study the hymns in Amos' book: 4:13, 5:8-9, and 9:5-6. What do they tell you about God?

4. Make a list of all the wrong attitudes and actions that Amos mentions, and take stock of your own life. Then pray for your nation.

5. Study the place of the Jews in God's plan of salvation, Romans 9-12.

6. Study other promise oracles about Israel's restoration, such as Hosea 2:21-23, 14:1-9; Isaiah 2:1-5, 4:2-6, 25:6-12, 35:1-10, 49:8-26, 56:1-8, and 60:1-66:24. Find others in Jeremiah, Ezekiel, Zechariah, and the other prophets.

7. Using the word *day*, find other references to "the day of the LORD" in the Old and New Testaments. What will happen on that day?

8. Go back through the book of Amos and choose key verses to memorize and meditate upon.

9. Read about the fulfillment of Amos' prophecy in 2 Kings 14:23-17:41.

STUDY AIDS

For further information on the material covered in this study, consider the following sources. If your local bookstore does not have them, you can have the bookstore order them from the publishers, or you can find them in most seminary libraries. Many college and public libraries will also carry these books.

Commentaries on Amos

Boice, James Montgomery. "Amos" in *The Minor Prophets: Volume 1: Hosea-Jonah* (Zondervan, 1983).

Based on some of Boice's sermons, this book is homiletical and full of good applications for modern Americans. A thoroughly evangelical outlook. Boice emphasizes the current relevance of Amos and explains some difficult theological issues, such as the place of the Jews in God's plan.

Martin-Achard, Robert, and S. Paul Re'emi. *God's People in Crisis: Amos and Lamentations* (Eerdmans, 1984).

The International Theological Commentary series is just that—written by authors from all over the world, and emphasizing the Bible's theological relevance today. Some might find Martin-Achard's work on Amos a bit liberal or sophisticated, but his insights are deep and he is committed to all of Scripture as God's reliable Word to us. This is a brief paperback and well worth reading.

Matthew Henry's Commentary on the Whole Bible: Volume 4: Jeremiah to Malachi (Revell, 1979).

A classic exposition of the book of Amos, first published in 1712 and still used for sermon preparation and daily devotions by many Christians. Henry's applications are illuminating, and his use of other scriptures and quotations is most helpful.

Mays, James L. *Amos: A Commentary* (Westminster, 1969).

Currently regarded as the standard critical commentary for English readers, this book is helpful for serious students, but many people will object to its somewhat liberal assertions about parts of Amos that were written by later men. However, Mays competently explains the meaning of the text in clear, nontechnical language. His purpose is interpretation, not application.

Motyer, J. A. *The Day of the Lion: The Message of Amos* (InterVarsity, 1974).

The Voice of the Old Testament series is an effort by evangelical scholars to let God speak through Old Testament books to modern people. Motyer's exposition of Amos is superb at explanation and application, and it is based on thorough study. Motyer's analysis is startling at some points, but he illuminates the book brilliantly.

Old Testament History and Culture

A ***history*** or ***survey*** traces Israel's history from beginning to end, so that you can see where each biblical event fits. *A Survey of Israel's History* by Leon Wood (Zondervan, 1970) is a good basic introduction for laymen from a conservative viewpoint. Not critical or heavily learned, but not simplistic. Many other good histories are available.

A ***Bible dictionary*** or ***Bible encyclopedia*** alphabetically lists articles about people, places, doctrines, important words, customs, and geography of the Bible.

The New Bible Dictionary, edited by J.D. Douglas, F.F. Bruce, J.I. Packer, N. Hillyer, D. Gutherie, A.R. Millard, and D.J. Wiseman (Tyndale, 1982) is more comprehensive than most dictionaries. Its 1300 pages include quantities of information along with excellent maps, charts, diagrams, and an index for cross-referencing.

Unger's Bible Dictionary by Merrill F. Unger (Moody, 1979) is equally excellent and is available in an inexpensive paperback edition.

The Zondervan Pictorial Encyclopedia edited by Merrill C. Tenney (Zondervan, 1975, 1976) is excellent and exhaustive. It is being revised and updated in the 1980s. However, its five 1000-page volumes are a financial investment, so all but very serious students may prefer to use it at a library.

A good ***Bible atlas*** can be a great aid to understanding what is going on in a book of the Bible and how geography affected events. Here are a few good choices:

The MacMillan Atlas by Yohanan Aharoni and Michael Avi-Yonah (MacMillan, 1968, 1977) contains 264 maps, 89 photos, and 12 graphics. The many maps of individual events portray battles, movements of people, and changing boundaries in detail.

The *New Bible Atlas* by J.J. Bimson and J.P. Kane (Tyndale, 1985) has 73 maps, 34 photos, and 34 graphics. Its evangelical perspective, concise and helpful text, and excellent research make it a very good choice, but its greatest strength is its outstanding graphics, such as cross-sections of the Dead Sea.

The *Bible Mapbook* by Simon Jenkins (Lion, 1984) is much shorter and less expensive than most other atlases, so it offers a good first taste of the usefulness of maps. It contains 91 simple maps, very little text, and 20 graphics. Some of the graphics are computer-generated and intriguing.

The Moody Atlas of Bible Lands by Barry J. Beitzel (Moody, 1984) is scholarly, very evangelical, and full of theological text, indexes, and references. This admirable reference work will be too deep and costly for some, but Beitzel shows vividly how God prepared the land of Israel perfectly for the acts of salvation He was going to accomplish in it.

Yohanan Aharoni has also written *The Land of the Bible: A Historical Geography* (Westminster Press, 1967). After describing the mountains, deserts, winds, rains, and trade routes of ancient Palestine, Aharoni traces the Old Testament history of the promised land with maps and text. For instance, he shows how Abraham lived in Beersheba and how different Judah was from Galilee.

A ***handbook*** of bible customs can also be useful. Some good ones are *Today's Handbook of Bible Times and Customs* by William L. Coleman (Bethany, 1984) and the less detailed *Daily Life in Bible Times* (Nelson, 1982).

Old Testament Words

A ***concordance*** lists words of the Bible alphabetically along with each verse in which the word appears. It lets you do your own word studies. An *exhaustive* concordance lists every instance of every word in a given translation. An *abridged* or *complete* concordance omits either some words, some occurrences of the word, or both.

The two best exhaustive concordances are *Strong's Exhaustive Concordance* and *Young's Analytical Concordance to the Bible.* Both are based on the King James Version of the Bible. *Strong's* has an index by which you can find out which Greek or Hebrew word is used in a given English verse. *Young's* breaks up each English-word listing according to the Greek or Hebrew words it translates. Thus, you can cross-reference the original language's words without knowing that language.

Among other good, less expensive concordances, *Cruden's Complete Concordance* is keyed to the King James and Revised Versions, and *The NIV Complete Concordance* is keyed to the New International Version. These include all references to every word included, but they omit "minor" words. They also lack indexes to the original languages.

The Expository Dictionary of the Old Testament, edited by Merrill F. Unger and William White (Thomas Nelson, 1980) defines major biblical Hebrew words. It is not exhaustive, but it is adequate for the average Bible student who does not know Hebrew.

For Small Group Leaders

How to Lead Small Group Bible Studies (NavPress, 1982).
Just 71 pages. It hits the highlights of how to get members acquainted, ask questions, plan lessons, deal with interpersonal relations, and handle prayer.

The Small Group Leader's Handbook by Steve Barker et. al. (InterVarsity, 1982).
Written by an InterVarsity small group with college students primarily in mind. It includes more than the above book on small group dynamics and how to lead in light of them, and many ideas for worship, building community, and outreach. It has a good chapter on doing inductive Bible study.

Getting Together: A Guide for Good Groups by Em Griffin (InterVarsity, 1982).
Applies to all kinds of groups, not just Bible studies. From his own experience, Griffin draws deep insights into why people join groups; how people relate to each other; and principles of leadership, decision-making, and discussions. It is fun to read, not highbrow, but its 229 pages will take more time than the above books.

You Can Start a Bible Study Group by Gladys Hunt (Harold Shaw, 1984).
Builds on Hunt's thirty years of experience leading groups. This book is wonderfully focused on God's enabling. It is both clear and applicable for Bible study groups of all kinds.

The Small Group Letter (NavPress).
Unique. Its six pages per issue, ten issues per year are packed with practical ideas for asking questions, planning Bible studies, leading discussion, dealing with group dynamics, encouraging spiritual growth, doing outreach, and so on. It stays up to date because writers always discuss what they are currently doing as small group members and leaders. To subscribe, write to Subscription Services, Post Office Box 1164, Dover, New Jersey 07801.

Bible Study Methods

Braga, James. *How to Study the Bible* (Multnomah, 1982).
Clear chapters on a variety of approaches to Bible study: synthetic, geographical, cultural, historical, doctrinal, practical, and so on. Designed to help the ordinary person without seminary training to use these approaches.

Fee, Gordon, and Douglas Stuart. *How to Read the Bible For All Its Worth* (Zondervan, 1982).

After explaining in general what interpretation (exegesis) and application (hermeneutics) are, Fee and Stuart offer chapters on interpreting and applying the different kinds of writing in the Bible: Epistles, Gospels, Old Testament Law, Old Testament narrative, the Prophets, Psalms, Wisdom, and Revelation. Fee and Stuart also suggest good commentaries on each biblical book. They write as conservative scholars who personally recognize Scripture as God's Word for their daily lives.

Jensen, Irving L. *Independent Bible Study* (Moody, 1963), and *Enjoy Your Bible* (Moody, 1962).

The former is a comprehensive introduction to the inductive Bible study method, especially the use of synthetic charts. The latter is a simpler introduction to the subject.

Wald, Oletta. *The Joy of Discovery in Bible Study* (Augsburg, 1975).

Wald focuses on issues such as how to observe all that is in a text, how to ask questions of a text, how to use grammar and passage structure to see the writer's point, and so on. Very helpful on these subjects.